7 Winning Conflict Resolution Techniques

MASTER NONVIOLENT AND EFFECTIVE COMMUNICATION SKILLS TO RESOLVE EVERYDAY CONFLICTS IN THE WORKPLACE, RELATIONSHIPS, MARRIAGE, AND CRUCIAL CONVERSATIONS

GERARD SHAW

FREE GIFT

This book includes a bonus booklet. Download may be for a limited time only. All information on how you can secure your gift right now can be found at the end of this book.

TABLE OF CONTENTS

Understanding the World of Conflict

Stages of Conflict

Causes of Conflict

    Professional Conflict

    Relationship and Interpersonal Relationship Conflict

    Personal Conflict

Chapter Summary

Foundations of Conflict Resolution

Stronger Relationships

Goal Achievement and Success

Showing Excellent Leadership and Team Management Skills

Embracing New Perspectives

Conflict Resolution Theories

    Conflict Theory One: Morton Deutsch - Cooperative Model

    Conflict Theory Two: Roger Fisher and William Ury

    Conflict Theory Three: John Burton - Human Needs Model

    Conflict Theory Four: Bush, Folger and Lederach

INTRODUCTION

Why is conflict resolution so important? In this book, you will learn that conflict and conflict resolution skills are crucial to your success and personal growth. Everybody experiences conflict throughout their life. Conflict happens because everyone is unique. We all interpret and communicate ideas differently, and we don't always have the same priority or point of view. Conflict can be looked at as unhealthy and harmful, and it can often stress us out and lower our happiness and productivity. However, when we use conflict to develop better understandings with those around us, it can be a positive experience. This is because conflict can teach you a lot about yourself and give you tools to use in your daily life.

This book was written to help people like you who are unsure of how to address conflict. Do you avoid conflict and confrontation? Have you always struggled with communicating your ideas to others? Do your conflicts always escalate out of control? Do you wish you experienced more positive outcomes from the conflicts in your life? In the first two chapters of this book, you will learn about what conflict is, what causes it, and how we each deal with it in our own way. The remainder of the book provides you with seven techniques that are explained in detail so you can approach and resolve any conflict with confidence.

These seven techniques are:

1. Mastering the power of conversation through verbal communication tools.

2. Mastering the power of conversation through non-verbal communication tools.

3. Managing emotions.

4. Changing minds through persuasion and negotiation.

5. Developing emotional intelligence so you can resolve conflict like a leader.

6. The strategy of peace.

7. The power of keeping an open mind.

The seven techniques in this book are presented in a general and well-rounded way so you can customize our techniques to your situation. Examples are used to illustrate concepts so you are able to put the information in context. Part of the reason why conflict can be difficult to resolve is that we are stuck in our own minds and insist on getting our point across. There are many more points of view to consider than just your own. By using empathy and effective listening, we can engage with others in a more positive way. Dedication, self-reflection, and the techniques presented in this book will give you the knowledge to better understand conflict and what causes it. You will be able to identify your own triggers and how you contribute to dispute. Often, we don't realize that we are contributing to the problem. This book was designed to help you take a step back, manage your emotions, motivate you towards success, and resolve conflicts with confidence. Our methods are easy to follow so that you can learn quickly and practice them whenever you need them.

This book will help you to understand conflict within yourself, how to recognize pending conflicts, how you contribute to conflict with others, and what environmental factors play a role in helping resolution. By the time you are finished reading this book, you will have a different perspective about conflict and conflict resolution than you do now. If you are tired of conflicts in your relationships and within yourself, why wait longer to resolve them? Rather than procrastinating, you can start fixing the problem by reading more right now. All the tools you need are provided in this book so that in any situation you face you will know what to say, how to say it, and how to achieve a more positive outcome. By reading this book and using our seven techniques, you will be better equipped to solve problems and resolve conflict in your own life.

This book comes with a FREE booklet on masterminding a winning routine to improve calmness and your level of confidence daily. Head to the bottom of this book for instructions on how you can secure your copy today.

CHAPTER ONE

Understanding the World of Conflict

What is conflict? Conflict usually occurs when two or more individuals disagree on a subject and the disagreement leads to anger, hostility, or animosity. A difference of perception, beliefs or opinions is often at the forefront of conflict. However, you can also be in conflict with yourself. You may be questioning your perceptions or beliefs, or you might be unsure about the decisions you need to make. You may be in conflict with yourself as a result of a conflict with someone else. Three of the main discussion topics that most often lead to conflict are: money, religion, and politics. These topics can be described in terms of economics, values, and power.

Economic Conflict: There are a limited amount of resources available to the groups or individuals involved. Each individual has their own opinion about how to ration the limited resources. The individuals discuss or debate about the allocation of wealth or assets. When they cannot agree, the issue escalates into a conflict between the parties.

5

Value Conflict: These conflicts typically occur when someone's beliefs and morals are in conflict with someone else's. The argument often centers around behavior, religion, culture, or social issues. One party wants the other party or parties to believe or behave in a way that conforms to a social norm that they believe is superior. The refusal of either party to change can escalate into conflict.

Power Conflict: Power conflicts arise mainly in the political and organizational arenas, with authoritative public figures or groups. However, power conflicts can also exist between individuals on a personal level. When political values differ, or one person or group tries to dominate decision making on behalf of other parties, that can lead to conflict.

Whether the conflict is based on economics, values, or power, getting to the root of what caused the conflict is the first step towards finding resolution. When you understand what the conflict is about and why it escalated, you are more likely to succeed in resolving or diffusing the problematic situation. Whether conflict happens within us or with others, when we take a step back and evaluate the root causes of the conflict, we learn about the boundaries of others and ourselves.

Many people look at conflict as a bad thing, but it can be a positive thing. Conflict is negative and unhealthy when the people in the conflict feel attacked, violated, unheard, misled or misunderstood. What makes conflict healthy is the willingness to resolve it. Conflict is positive when it leads to both parties deciding to agree to disagree or to compromise to diffuse the situation.

There are very unhealthy ways to address conflict, and this is what most people resort to when handling stressful affairs. Some people have underlying characteristics such as anger issues, a superiority complex, narcissistic or sociopathic tendencies. This drives them to act and behave impulsively, or react with hostility and resentment when confronted. Other people may have grown up in an environment where conflict was resolved in a negative or hurtful way, so they emulate this behavior. Some people avoid conflict altogether. Some of the unhealthy ways people deal with conflict are listed below.

Avoidance and Denial: Avoidance or denial is used when people remove themselves from the situation and refuse to discuss or resolve it. They will often pretend there is no issue, and say things like "everything is fine" or "there's no problem" when asked about the topic. This rarely leads to resolution. The problem doesn't go away. Instead, it lingers in the background and festers, turning into a larger argument later.

Blaming: This occurs when one party accuses the other party of being at fault for the situation Blaming stems from anger and personal insecurities, and it only escalates the conflict further. The person who is blaming thinks that they are diffusing the situation by making the other take responsibility for their actions. This can be perceived as an attack and cause the other person to be defensive, refuse to accept blame and blame the other party in return. This can escalate quickly and lead to heated fights.

Power and Influence: Trying to resolve conflict in this way means that parties compete to "win" at the other's expense. The primary purpose is to win the argument rather than see the other's perspective. Negative behaviors may be used to convince the other party to give up or cause them to lose. Tactics include threats to job security, using things against one another, making complaints, sabotage, etc. When someone "wins," they may think the fight is over; however, the "loser" will likely be resentful, fearful, or sad.

Manipulation: Manipulation comes in many forms, such as brainwashing, gaslighting, control of assets, passive-aggressiveness, guilt-trips, and inequitable compromise. Manipulators are just trying to resolve a situation to their benefit and their perceived efforts at resolution are usually self-serving. Examples of manipulative behavior include the following scenarios: An individual proposes an idea but makes it seem like it was the other person's idea in order to increase the chance of it being accepted; A compromise may be proposed that is not fair to one party, but if that party refuses they look like they are not being cooperative; Someone might say, "If you were truly loyal, you would do X for me."

Stages of Conflict

Conflict can be both positive and negative, and it can have both positive and negative outcomes. A positive way to approach conflict is by learning from the situation. From a positive perspective, we need conflict to help us develop our problem-solving skills and for our personal growth. The outcome can be positive when parties come to an

8

amicable agreement. The conflict can be negative if we choose to deal with it in an aggressive way. The outcome is negative if the conflict results in the destruction of a relationship. Whether or not the conflict is positive or negative, there are common stages to all conflicts.

The five stages of conflict are:

1. The latent stage.

2. The perceived stage.

3. The felt stage.

4. The manifest stage.

5. The aftermath stage.

The **latent phase** of conflict means that something is happening that will lead to an adverse situation later, but no one realizes it. For example, your roommate asks you to pick up some shampoo and conditioner from the store for them since you are going to the store anyway. When you get to the store, you select and buy some shampoo and conditioner, not knowing that they wouldn't ever use that brand. This is the latent stage in the conflict. Neither of you knew there would be a problem stemming from this transaction.

The **perceived stage** of conflict is when both parties or the group of individuals know and understand that there is a conflict happening. When you come home with the hair products, an argument happens because she does not like the brand you bought her and she doesn't want to keep it. You think she should be happy with what you selected since she did not specify what she wanted. Similarly, if two employees are working on a project together, they might have different ideas about what needs to be done. No one is willing to compromise and they start to argue about which plan to support.

In the **felt stage**, emotions like anxiety, nervousness or anger are felt by one or all of the individuals in the conflict. In the example with the roommates, the felt stage happens when both individuals are heated due to the miscommunication and subsequent accusation about the shampoo and conditioner. Your roommate is annoyed because she assumed you knew which type to buy because you share the same shower. You are upset that she's ungrateful about the favor you did her.

In the **manifest stage**, the conflict is now in progress and it is either escalating or attempts to resolve it are being made. In the example of the two roommates, after arguing for a while, they agree to either do their own shopping, or to be more specific about what they want. In the workplace, if the conflict escalates between two employees, they might ask a manager which approach best suits the client's needs.

The last stage is the **aftermath**. This happens after the previous stages take their course, and the problem becomes resolved one way or another. With the examples of the roommates and the workplace, both conflicts had a positive aftermath. A negative aftermath would have been if the roommates' fight escalated to the point they could no longer cohabitate, or one of the employees quit because they could not tolerate not getting their way.

In addition to understanding the stages of conflict, it's important to understand the different types of conflict. There are five basic types of conflict.

1. Conflict within yourself.

2. Interpersonal conflict.

3. The conflict between a person and a group.

4. Inter-group conflict.

5. Inter-organizational conflict.

The first type of conflict is **conflict within yourself**. This usually means that you are considering violating a value, boundary, or moral that you hold dear, or that you have a difficult decision to make. Perhaps you are considering another person's opinion and you don't know how to react. Perhaps you are both honest and loyal, and a friend asks you to lie for them. That would compromise your values and you might be conflicted by your desire to be both honest and loyal to your friend. You might be wondering if they are truly your friend if they would ask you to be dishonest on their behalf. These are significant inner conflicts.

The next type of conflict is **interpersonal**. This type of conflict is probably the most common type of conflict, and it happens between two or more people. An example of this would be that two people share the same love interest, and both are competing for that person's attention. Another example can be found in the workplace. Three people may be up for a promotion, and all are equally deserving of the position but only one person can get it. This causes conflict between coworkers as they

11

compete and when one "wins". It may also cause conflict between the employees and the employer who is responsible for making the decision.

The third type of conflict arises when there is a **conflict between one person and a group**. The conflict between a group and an individual happens when one person doesn't agree with the rest of the group's position but wants to get along due to the benefits of being in the group. For example, if you are at a book club and you get constructive criticism about your ideas, you may not agree with the group. You can only stay if you can get along, so you must decide if the disagreement is important enough to impact your overall participation. Another example is being part of a group that is arguing because some people want to create a petition for something, but you don't think it's a good use of the group's time.

Inter-group conflict arises mostly in the workplace and with businesses and companies. For example, there may be conflict within a company if a new CEO and management team are hired to reorganize. When they come in with ideas on how to create a new division of the company, the people who have been at the company long term may not welcome the newcomers' ideas. This can cause conflict between groups of personnel.

Inter-organizational conflict mainly happens between two organizations such as buyers and suppliers, unions and companies, government agencies and advocacy groups. These organizations may run differently from each other or have different priorities about what should happen or how things should operate.

Conflict can be personal or professional. It can be between two people or two conglomerates. It can be small scale or large scale. No matter what, we are likely to encounter conflict in our lives. Identifying and understanding the underlying reasons for conflict is an important aspect of conflict resolution.

Causes of Conflict

There are many causes of conflict. Understanding the root causes of conflict is essential to having positive outcomes and avoiding mistakes. We know that the big picture causes of conflict are typically related to economics, values, and power. Regardless of what people argue about, there are many actions and behaviors that commonly lead to the initiation or escalation of conflict. These common causes of conflict are:

- Miscommunication.

- Lack of information.

- Misinterpretation.

- Different perspectives.

- Destructive thought patterns.

- The inability to regulate our emotions.

These things can influence the development of a conflict whether it is at work, in your relationships or within yourself. The most common way of preventing a conflict before it begins is to be aware of yourself and your surroundings. We can control our reactions and behaviors. When problems arise, it's usually because emotions have been allowed to run high without pausing and taking a step back from the whole situation. Many people struggle with this because they aren't aware of how they are feeling, they are emotionally impulsive or they fail to recognize the signs around them. Here are more examples of the causes of conflict in the various areas of our lives:

Professional Conflict

- Manipulation tactics used to climb the company ladder.

- Competition for recognition, promotion or raises.

- Not enough growth within a company or organization.

- Different beliefs about how management should act.

- Deadline constraints.

- Lack of information between different groups.

- Difference in opinions and thought process.

Relationship and Interpersonal Relationship Conflict

- Heightened emotions.

- Judgment or labeling.

- Defensive or offensive ways of communicating.

- Poor communication skills.

- Mixed signals.

- Pessimistic behavior.

Personal Conflict

- When an action doesn't match a moral or personal value.

- Different opinions or beliefs from someone else.

- Being in a compromised situation.

- Identity crisis - or not knowing oneself fully.

Once we recognize the stages and causes of a conflict, we are more fully equipped to address it and influence its outcome.

Chapter Summary

As you have learned, conflict and its resolution are more complicated than most think. In this chapter, we were able to identify what conflict is and how it starts. More of what was covered in this chapter includes:

- Unhealthy ways of dealing with conflict.

- The stages of conflict.

- The causes of conflict.

- The types of conflict.

In the subsequent chapters, you will first learn about the foundations of conflict resolution, and then we will dive into the seven techniques of conflict resolution and learn how to put them into practice.

CHAPTER TWO

Foundations of Conflict Resolution

Before we dive into the seven techniques for resolving conflict, we must first learn about the foundations of conflict resolution. Conflict resolution isn't just about being aware and staying patient with yourself and with the person you are in conflict with. It's about learning to read someone's behavior, tap into your emotions, and figuring out the best problem-solving skills to use at the right moment. The foundations of conflict resolution include knowing the signs of conflict before it happens, what to do during the conflict, and how to respond to the aftermath of an argument.

Everyone has their own way of dealing with conflict and coming up with solutions, and no two conflicts are the same because no two people or situations are identical. Conflict resolution is an important life skill because it can help you to maneuver more easily through life, to become more successful and to be more graceful and professional in difficult situations. You might think that conflict resolution requires that you never lose your temper. Wrong. We are all human, and we all make mistakes, say things we don't mean, and forget what we have been

17

practicing from time to time. To be able to resolve conflict doesn't mean that you can never speak out or lose your temper. Sometimes, we must be assertive about our opinion to get our point across. However, conflict resolution teaches us how to avoid losing our cool in a way that hurts others or compromises the resolution of the difficult situation.

People who struggle with fighting and violence may have an underlying problem with handling challenging environments or confrontation because they cannot separate their own beliefs and opinions from those of others. When someone can identify their conflict triggers, they can learn how to cope with or prepare for any confrontation. When you understand what the root cause of the problem is, you can easily take a step back and work toward creative problem-solving, team building and long-term relationships. This requires you to figure out what your typical response to conflict is, and when it usually kicks in. Learning how to resolve confrontation quickly has many benefits, some of which are discussed below.

Stronger Relationships

Most strong, positive relationships are built on trust, loyalty, reliability, boundaries, and respect. When you learn how to resolve conflict and understand where it comes from, you can build healthier relationships. Honesty, healthy boundaries, and personal assertiveness are at the root of strong relationships. Not all conflict is wrong or unhealthy, and it can be okay to argue or have healthy disagreements. This is because to build relationships you need to understand the other person's perspective.

18

For example, one person might need to find a roommate, so they post an ad online. You see it, and everything they offer sounds incredible so you respond to it, and after a couple of weeks you are all moved in. After some time has passed, a conflict arises because they brought home a dog. You are allergic and have told them before that you are allergic to pet hair. They defied your wishes because they didn't think you would be home at the time and that it wouldn't be a big deal. As a result, an argument breaks out. After arguing for a while, your roommate takes the dog for a walk until the owner can come to pick it up. When they come home, you have a healthy and calm talk. The roommate says that they didn't realize you were so allergic and that in the future they will never bring an animal home. You believe that they are sincere and that they can be trusted. Hence the relationship grows, and you build a closer and stronger friendship.

Goal Achievement and Success

Conflict resolution skills can have a real impact on your ability to succeed and achieve your goals. When you switch your mindset, learn new ways to view things, learn body language cues and effective listening strategies, you are better equipped to face all challenges. Conflict resolution involves being aware of how you speak, how your message is perceived, and how to present the right message. This takes self-awareness. You cannot just see confrontation coming and immediately know how to handle it. You need to know what the other party is thinking or feeling. These skills take time, dedication, and motivation to master. This perseverance and self-discipline are key to successfully setting and achieving goals.

Showing Excellent Leadership and Team Management Skills

Conflict resolution skills help you to look at situations in a way that views every confrontation as "us" instead of "me." A leader thinks of others and how decisions will affect the team. A good leader shows empathy for others and tries to understand how decisions will impact those around them. Leading others effectively requires commitment and dedication to follow through with actions once they say they will do something. Conflict resolution skills set you up for leadership and for being a stronger part of a team.

Embracing New Perspectives

Our perspectives greatly influence our actions. Some people are stubborn, and others are flexible. Some people are short-tempered while others are patient. Some people are closed-minded while others are open-minded. Conflict resolution skills help you define who you are and how you perceive and respond to dispute. It's about learning how others feel and think and about being open to learning new points of view. Conflict resolution gives you further insight into how to combine your perspective with the views of others so that an equitable outcome can be achieved.

It's true that we cannot avoid conflict, and that it is likely to come into our lives at some point. Most times conflict is seen as a bad thing because it triggers strong emotions. However, conflict can be positive since it is an opportunity to grow as an individual. Embrace change and be open to the perspectives of others.

Conflict Resolution Theories

Throughout history, there have been many theories about conflict resolution. Four of the major theories are discussed below.

Conflict Theory One: Morton Deutsch - Cooperative Model

The first theory is the Cooperative Model by Morton Deutsch. His theory is based on interpersonal relationships being motivated by either cooperation or competition. The cooperative process allows us to resolve disputes by being willing and open to another person's ideas and views. This has a positive effect. Competition however, means that two parties cannot cooperate because of the inner motive to compete and win. Deutch's theory says that almost always, competition in a conflict will have a negative consequence with one person coming out as the "winner" and the other as a "loser". His research suggests that constructive conflict resolution results from a cooperative nature and a desire to resolve problems. Deutch concluded that if both parties are cooperative, they can more easily come to an understanding of each other's views. He believed this could be achieved by learning the norms of cooperation. These norms are honesty, respect, acknowledgment, empathy, forgiveness, and a mutual understanding of the situation and the conflict.

21

Conflict Theory Two: Roger Fisher and William Ury - Principled Negotiation

In the Principled Negotiation Theory, Fisher and Ury were brought together at Harvard University to work on a project called "The Negotiation Project". In 1943, Fisher studied Law at the University and took on the interest of solving people's disputes. He was impressed by Ury's research paper on Middle East peace negotiations and invited Ury to work with him after he became a professor at Harvard in 1960. Together, they wrote the book "Getting to Yes" which quickly became a best-seller. Working with Fisher and his teachings, Ury became a mediator and negotiation advisor.

The Principled Negotiation Theory discussed in "Getting to Yes" discusses how to achieve a good negotiation outcome. They believed that people are problem-solvers and that a good agreement is wise and efficient. This means that it satisfies the interests of both parties. In their findings, Fisher and Ury set out four essential principles for how to make negotiation effective. They were to separate the person (or people) from the problem (or conflict); to focus on agendas, not situations; to create ideas for mutual understanding; and to use objective guidelines. The focus of this theory was to have each conflicted party (person) achieve agreement and compromise by negotiating on those terms.

Conflict Theory Three: John Burton - Human Needs Model

Burton's Human Needs Model is based on the belief that conflict is a social matter or a personal problem related to human needs. Burton says if social inequity is the root cause of conflict, then it is irrelevant to try to solve it until social norms are corrected. Burton suggests that social norms would have to be adjusted to suit the needs of every individual. He believes that aggression and antisocial behavior stems from social circumstances and the denial of human needs. He concludes that in order to stop future conflicts and damaging behavior social changes must be achieved, for example, employees must be given recognition, and teenagers must be given a role in society. Burton suggests that it isn't the people who need to change for society, but the society that needs to change for people.

Conflict Theory Four: Bush, Folger and Lederach - Conflict Transformation

The Conflict Transformation Theory suggests that instead of trying to resolve or manage conflict, we should transform it. Transformation requires a solution that satisfies the interests of all groups. Bush, Folger, and Lederach's idea of conflict transformation requires changing an individual's attitude and behavior and the relationship between two or more conflicting parties. Lederach suggested that by focusing on mutual needs and understanding, instead of the differences between the parties, we are more likely to transform conflict into dialogue and be empowered to resolve issues cooperatively.

Now that we understand some major theories of conflict resolution, let's look at how to identify our own behaviors and responses to conflict.

Problem-Solving Behaviors

When we look at people's behaviors, we observe how they act in various situations, their values, personality, and characteristics. So, what exactly are problem-solving or conflict resolving behaviors? These are behaviors that people have when they try to diffuse an awkward encounter or solve an issue. Assertiveness is one of the most common behaviors people use when they are in conflict. Other common types of behaviors people exhibit when dealing with confrontation or dispute are:

- Accommodating roles.

- Avoidance.

- Compromising.

- Collaborating.

- Competition.

The **accommodating** response is when people put aside all their needs and wants for those of others. While this may seem like a good approach, it can actually be hurtful as the accommodating individual may feel as though they are unable to get what they want from the situation. This can lead to or stem from a lack of confidence or self-esteem. Although this might be good behavior to diffuse a situation or prevent an issue from escalating in the short term, it can be used as a form of avoidance or in order to push the root problem aside. The only times where this method may be useful is when the issue is not that important to you, or if you have been manipulated or pushed to agree and you don't want to fight anymore. Sometimes, it can be used in order to gracefully exit a situation.

The **avoidance** behavior signifies fear or lack of responsibility in most cases. The avoidance technique is to either pretend there is no conflict, ignore the issue, or procrastinate until the problem "fixes itself." This type of conflict resolving behavior is perhaps the most inefficient way of handling conflict. It can stem from fear of confrontation, or if the person feels as though they are too superior to handle such "petty" issues. This approach may be used if someone believes they can't "win" the argument anyway, or if they are waiting for more information to bolster their case.

A **compromise** can be efficient and effective when both parties come out equally on top. It's a positive behavior based on finding a middle ground or something that each party is willing to lose in order to gain something else. This is best when the dispute is between two people rather than a large group. A compromise can be effective if the goal is to reach a mutually agreeable solution. A compromise can be difficult to attain if both parties refuse to adjust their position.

Collaboration behaviors include the expectation that everyone wins. If this isn't possible, the conflict resolution may result in compromise and negotiation strategies. This type of behavior is perhaps the most rewarding method to resolve conflict as it helps everyone to work together and see eye-to-eye. Everyone wins and everyone benefits. This will often result in both parties getting everything they need, since each party helps the other with their goals.

Competition is only positive behavior when it's fun and friendly, such as minor gambling, friendly bets, games, sports, or races. Other

25

means of competing, such as with your partner for an interest that only one individual can gain is negative behavior. The competition behavior is common in an argumentative person that always has to get the last word in. Even though you address their issues, prove your point, and define your concerns, you still lose in their eyes due to their competitiveness. They want to "one-up" someone else or prove their point without hearing anyone else's.

Everyone has their own ways of managing an awkward situation. Some people are more aggressive than others, while some people give up trying to win. Effective conflict resolution sometimes requires you to "pick your battles". Sometimes, we are not in a position to win, or we don't have time to argue. We need to learn when to speak and when not to speak, as well as when to listen. In all cases, we need to approach problem solving and conflict resolution with positive intent, using principles such as openness, empathy, equality, and positivity.

Openness

To be open means to have an "open mind". This requires us to listen effectively before responding out of emotional impulse and to take the time to truly consider the viewpoint of the other person. Your main goal is to recognize their viewpoint, state your true feelings and then work together to identify the root problem and an effective solution. Using "I feel" and "How do you feel about…?" statements and questions can help you to be more open in conflict situations.

Empathy

Empathy means truly trying to understand the experience, perspective, and feelings of the other party. It requires that you listen intently with the objective of understanding their point of view. You must put aside all judgments or previous notions about the party that you are in conflict with. You must truly try to be compassionate about their experience or viewpoint. An empathetic statement such as, "I didn't realize I made you feel that way" can help, or "I didn't realize this decision would have that outcome for you." If you are empathetic without being ingenuine, use positive language without using condescending tones, then it can show the person that you understand their needs and really do want to solve the issue.

Equality

Treat people as if they are equal to you. Many people say they know what equality means, yet they look down on the homeless, or resent their bosses or people that are different from them. The truth is that there will always be someone tougher, stronger, smarter, or wealthier than you, but you will also be tougher, stronger, smarter, or wealthier than someone else. Equality means that all judgments are put to rest, and you see others as having the same value as you regardless of their economic or social status. To practice this, consider everyone's ideas on the basis of merit only.

Positivity

If you approach issues with a negative mindset, and bring negativity with you everywhere, you will be inherently pessimistic. When you opt for positivity and optimism, you bring everyone's spirits up and motivate yourself and each other to find solutions, instead of focusing on problems. To practice positivity, express your enthusiasm for finding a solution, and help others see that their opinions are not being dismissed.

If we behave in these positive ways, we can be sure to find a solution, build healthier relationships, and succeed at a faster rate than those who are destructive and negative. When you are known for finding solutions in a positive, painless, and efficient way, you will be more highly regarded by others, feel better about yourself, and obtain further opportunities in your career and life.

Chapter Summary

As you have learned by now, there are different approaches to conflict resolution. To have a successful outcome, conflict resolution requires a positive mindset and behavior. If your typical response to dispute is aggressive, or someone has ulterior motives, the conflict will escalate and end negatively for everyone involved. Each person is different, thinks their own way, has their own views, and acts according to what they think is right. By using positive strategies that consider the needs of all parties, we are more likely to find an equitable solution to our conflict.

In this chapter, you learned about the foundations of conflict management. Specifically, we covered:

- The benefits of conflict resolution.

28

- Four well-known conflict theories.

- Typical problem-solving behaviors and responses.

- How to approach and de-escalate conflict.

The next chapter is the first of seven techniques for how to master conflict resolution. You will learn how to send the right message using effective verbal communication. You will gain a deep understanding of the power of dialog and why some people are harder to talk to than others.

CHAPTER THREE

Conflict Resolution Technique 01 - Mastering the Power of Conversation Through Verbal Communication

There are four main forms of communication: verbal, non-verbal, written, and visual. Verbal is often argued to be the most essential way of communicating. When we think about verbal communication, what comes to our minds? It's talking to each other about interests or issues. There are endless potential topics of discussion. But, are we talking to each other or at each other? In today's day and age, people communicate through texts, emails, social media, or other written forms of communication. When we are with someone face-to-face, we are often also on our phones or digital devices. This stops us from listening effectively and we completely miss dialogue. Many people think dialogue is when two or more people have a discussion, each taking turns to speak. However, dialogue is not just about talking to each other. It's about understanding what is being communicated, and determining what the message behind the words used are. Verbal communication has many more components than just speaking aloud. It's about learning to listen, gaining insight, thinking before responding, and ultimately preventing conflict as efficiently as possible. When you combine verbal with non-verbal communication (which you will learn about in the next chapter), you can become a master at communication.

Verbal communication is the practice of listening to what is said, interpreting it in the way that the speaker is meaning to convey their message, and responding appropriately to their statement. Many people hear what is being said but don't listen to what they are hearing. Poor listening skills result in misinterpretation of the facts, which can lead to conflict. The problem is that most people aren't really listening to understand. They listen to respond, and they are too focused on the things they want to say rather than what was just said by the other person. The solution to this problem is to learn effective listening techniques and then focus on conveying your message in the terms they are speaking about.

The basic skills that you need for effective verbal communication are:

- Effective speaking
  - Choose the right words to convey your message. Who is your audience?
  - Use the correct tone and don't be condescending, dismissive or aggressive.
  - Respond specifically to what the other person said.

- ○ Make sure there are no mixed signals from contradictory statements.

- Context

  - ○ Know who you are speaking with and what is important to them.
  - ○ Understand the topic you are discussing. Collect more information if needed.
  - ○ Ensure the location and time is appropriate for the conversation.

- Active listening

  - ○ Be open-minded.
  - ○ Stay non-judgmental.
  - ○ Avoid thinking of a response until you've listened fully to the other person's statement.
  - ○ Be patient and take the time to listen. Ask questions if you need something clarified.
  - ○ Stay focused on the speaker. Don't watch the TV over their shoulder, check your phone or change the subject.
  - ○ Listen to the full sentence, not just single words you heard throughout the conversation. You could misunderstand the overall message.

Learning to converse effectively takes practice and patience. You can both speak and listen by asking questions based on things you don't understand. Asking questions also tells the speaker that you want to know more, that you are enthusiastic about understanding the message they are trying to convey, and that you respect their right to be heard. It also shows that you are willing to engage without redirecting the conversation to yourself, which also builds rapport and trust. The last step to mastering effective verbal communication is ending the conversation in a respectful matter. Once there is an opening for the conversation to end, such as a pause of some length, you can close the discussion with the appropriate closing words. This may include respectfully summarizing what's been said, or saying, "That was really interesting. I'm glad we had the chance to talk."

Effective Speaking

Part of verbal communication is learning how to speak effectively. Effective speaking is as much about patience and listening as it is about the words you use. One of the problems with today's society is that no one wants to take the time to listen to each other speak. We are all too busy listening to our own thoughts and trying to get them out quickly. We often don't take the time to think carefully about what we are about to say. With social media, networking, and promotion building, we may be conversing with each other, but we aren't talking, and our focus is not on the conversation. It is with ourselves. For example, when you go to a social outing you may have the intention of promoting yourself and your ideas. How many people go to a gathering just to learn about other people and listen to their perspective? Effective speaking starts with effective listening.

Part of speaking effectively requires "saying what you mean and meaning what you say". In other words, you have to be genuine and truthful, and follow up on the things you promised to do. Speaking effectively requires you to convey your message according to how you want your message to be acted on. If you want a positive reaction you will use encouraging tones and words. If you want help from others, you would use a questioning tone or word the question based on what type of feedback you are looking for. Effective speaking requires the proper word choice and tone of voice. Also important are your breathing, the pitch of your voice and the clarity of your message. Pacing of delivery and diversity of word choice also plays a significant role in speaking competently.

Word Choice

The words you use are the most important aspect of effective speaking, and they must be chosen carefully to ensure they have the desired effect. You must take into consideration the context of the situation and who you are talking to. You wouldn't choose the same hard to read, complicated words with a child or a foreigner as you would with an authoritative academic person or native language speaker. Consider your audience and use words you know they will understand. If you aren't sure, use smaller sentences and simple language to ensure everyone knows what you are saying. When using examples, describe situations they can relate to. Words should always be positive and empowering, rather than negative or condescending.

Tone of Voice

There is so much you can tell about a person's mood, motive, and attitude just by listening to the tone of their voice. For example, a reserved person might talk quietly and hesitantly. The pitch and tone used by the speaker suggest they are shy, lack confidence, and are looking for leadership. For a shy person, you would approach them with an empathetic and reassuring nature and use a calm, quiet voice to encourage them to listen to you.

On the other hand, someone who is more confident will have a firm and commanding tone of voice. This implies that they know what they are talking about and that they can take a leadership role. Consider how you speak to others. Do you seem shy, confident, or somewhere in between? The tone of your voice matters since it influences the impression you give to others and their willingness to listen to your point of view.

The Effect of Breathing

Emotions come out in our voices. If we are nervous or anxious, our breath will be short and we might hyperventilate, or our voice might come out cracked and hesitant. If we are comfortable, our breathing will remain steady and be even and calm, which will help our voice come out smoothly. Our breath influences our body language, as well. For example, if our breathing is sporadic, our posture is stiff, and our muscles feel tense, these body language cues send signals to our brain that make us anxious, disturbing the calm flow of our voices. Imagine if singers couldn't get over being shy and reserved when they got on stage in front of large crowds. They wouldn't sound as confident or as competent as they do in the studio when only a few individuals are present. Singers and public speakers practice their breathing and record themselves, so they can identify the voice mistakes they make and can fix them. Make sure you are taking deep, regular breaths to convey confidence when you speak. Breathing deep and steadily has a calming effect, which will help you be more relaxed, focused and able to moderate your speech. Breathing influences tone, pitch and volume. The topic of breathing will come up again later in the book, so remember what you have learned here, as it will be reinforced later. That's how important breathing is to effective speaking.

Volume

Choosing the volume of your voice determines how effectively you are heard. Breathing plays a significant role in how loudly or quietly you speak. When we breathe deeply, we are able to project our voices loudly, which is sometimes necessary. For example, when trying to be heard in a group or a large room, speaking quietly is ineffective. You want to project your voice to the back of the room. However, if you are talking to someone that is directly in front of you, you do not want to yell at them. Instead, you will bring your volume down to where only they can hear you, or to a volume that is not overly loud. It is easier to speak in a calm, low voice when we are breathing at a calm and steady rate.

Transparency and Clarity

Transparency and clarity often determine the level to which you are understood and trusted. It is essentially about sending mixed messages. We may mean one thing but imply something different, or we may explain something in such a complicated manner that the point is misunderstood. Are you pretending to be okay when you are actually upset? Are you "beating around the bush?" This leads to mixed messages. This makes it hard to resolve conflicts because no one is focused on the actual issues.

Silence and Pauses

To send the message you want to convey in an appropriate matter, you must combine strong speech and appropriate pauses. If you are constantly speaking, the other party does not have a chance to listen, process the information and then respond. Once you are finished with one idea or sentence, take a quick pause before continuing to your next point. This gives the other person time to think about what you have said. Look at the other person to see if they are about to respond. Give them a chance to speak if they want to.

Difficult Conversations

Most conflicts arise because of, or during difficult conversations. A difficult conversation is a discussion about a topic that is uncomfortable for an individual. Most people do not like to engage in difficult conversations for fear of the consequences and the unpredictability of the outcome. Usually, tough conversations stem from wondering what happened, heightened emotions, differences of opinion about beliefs or behaviors, or personal identity questions. Effective speaking and listening strategies can turn an escalated argument into a learning opportunity. One thing to always keep in mind when you are entering or enduring a tough discussion is that you cannot control anyone but yourself in a heated moment. This ultimately means that if you must take a moment to collect yourself, you should do so. Let's review three difficult situations and how to manage them for the benefit of all parties.

"What Happened?"

Usually, in the "what happened" conflict, one individual thinks they know everything about an event, the motives of the opposing party, and how they felt. A situation may escalate quickly due to a misunderstanding or hastily said words. For example, if you unintentionally said something out of anger to your friend, they might assume that you said it to hurt them, and might conclude that you are a spiteful person. Another "what happened" moment can occur when one person thinks it's all the other person's fault, or they think it's all their own fault. This can result in blame, rejection and upset. The "it's all my/your fault" method of thinking is hurtful because it makes someone feel bad and reinforces the belief that only one person is to blame.

A better way to look at the conflict is to admit that all parties played a part in the events that led to the disagreement. Figure out who is responsible for what stages of the event, without pointing out blame. In the heat of the moment, you may assume that you know all sides of the story. This approach is closed-minded, which gets you nowhere. Instead, you must hear each other out by using your active listening skills and trying to see from the other person's side. More than likely, they have perceived the situation differently than you. One thing to remember when beginning a difficult conversation is that you are entitled to your own feelings and thoughts but you can never predict or assume you know what's going on in someone else's head.

Heightened Emotions

Heightened emotions may include rage, upset, sadness or confusion. When emotions are heightened, it can be challenging to get past them and focus on listening to someone else. Irrational emotions are something that we need to work through before we can go into a complicated discussion. Otherwise, they will blind us from seeing the truth and understanding the other's point of view. The challenge of heightened emotions type conversations is that they are hard to de-escalate and we may ultimately blame the other party for making us feel the way we do. In these moments we are vulnerable and because we believe they are the reason for our problem, we feel as though it's their responsibility to fix it and make us feel better. Our mistake in this way of thinking is that we actually have total control over how we feel at all times. Rather than looking for sympathy or for someone else to calm us down, the power is in our own hands to self-soothe. When intense feelings are causing a difficult conversation to escalate, we may lash out with harsh words or avoid talking calmly with the individual that made us upset. Analyze your own feelings, identify the trigger for the heightened emotion, and discuss what made you upset without judgment or blame. This will help to diffuse the conflict.

Personal Identity

This type of conversation exists within ourselves. It's all about what we say to ourselves and how much we listen to our inner critic. It's about who we are and how we present ourselves to others. Personal identity affects how we view others and ourselves, and how we assume others see us. As a defense to the outside world, we may throw up defensive walls around ourselves or become reclusive, or we may be unpredictable as a way to protect an all-or-nothing self-image. If someone makes us question our identity or second-guess our opinions or actions, it can cause conflict within ourselves and with others. It is important to understand that having a difference of opinion with someone does not mean they are questioning your personal identity. We all want to be heard, seen, and appreciated.

Managing Difficult Conversations

Engaging in difficult conversations feels uncomfortable, and sometimes we avoid these types of discussions so that we don't have to face the consequences. However, the more we avoid things, the more we are going to have conflict in our lives because we don't learn how to solve problems effectively. During a dispute, we tend to say and do things before we have had time to think about it. This causes conflicts to escalate. If we continue to do things this way, we end up with a history of broken friendships, and the loss of partners and jobs. We teach our brains that it's better to defend ourselves so that we don't get hurt rather than train our minds on how to resolve an issue to the benefit of all parties.

41

The first step to managing a difficult conversation is to prepare yourself mentally. Commit to being calm and non-adversarial. Be willing to look within yourself to see how you contributed to the conflict. Ask yourself why you are having the debate and what you want out of it. Start the discussion at a good time and in an appropriate place. Start by introducing the conversation and stating what your intent is. Make sure you are calm and focused. Observe the other person for clear signs that they are ready for the discussion. Once you are both ready to commit to the conversation and to resolving the problem, you can continue with the tough discussion. Make sure that your thoughts are clear and write them down if necessary. One of the first mistakes people make when starting a difficult conversation is that they describe the conflict only from their perspective. Talking in a third-person point of view helps things run more smoothly because it puts a neutral tone on the conversation. Ask the other person what their perspective is and then pay full attention to the speaker when they respond. In any conflict, the goal is to discuss things in a mature and calm manner and focus on solving the problem. Once all thoughts are shared you can begin to figure out how to resolve the issue. Expect that there may be disagreements and understand that there might still be tension afterward. If no resolution is reached at the end of the discussion, you may want to consider leaving things alone for a while. Some time and distance can give both parties the chance to evaluate their positions.

Here are some positive ways to approach conflict and work through challenging conversations:

Stick to Having a Fact-based Discussion

When you stick to the facts it is easier to focus on the objective of the conversation which is to solve a problem or conflict. During the discussion, your intent should be focused both on listening to the other's point of view and to getting your point across. Each person should get the opportunity to state the facts as they understand them. Decide what you agree on, and agree to find out the true facts about the items that you don't agree on. The conversation should be strictly fact-based until it is resolved. After the problem is solved you can decide whether or not you want to discuss other topics.

Be Assertive Yet Empathetic

Sometimes we need to recognize that what we say may seem offensive or hurtful if it is misunderstood. When it is your turn to speak, and you know something may be interpreted as offensive or upsetting, start by introducing the potential conflict. For example, "What I am about to say might offend or upset you, and I don't mean to, so I apologize in advance. I feel xxx". Always be objective by stating how you feel while avoiding "you" statements which can be interpreted as blaming. The goal is to assert your opinions while also keeping in mind how others feel. Remember that what you say may lead to a greater conflict.

Stay Confident While Being Transparent

We seem more confident when we effectively use our voice at the correct volume and tone. When we are clear about our point of view and have anticipated the point of view of others, it is easier to confidently

43

get our point across. Going into the discussion with openness and transparency is practical because it causes us to get the point and be honest. Offer information freely and ask for the other person's opinion.

Don't Take Anything Personally

When involved in conflict we often take everything that is said to heart, which hurts our feelings and can cause us to respond irrationally. Listen objectively and try not to take what the other person is saying too personally. Try staying focused on the issue, and not on how it makes you feel to be in conflict. When resolving a conflict by having a difficult conversation, be truthful, listen effectively and leave sensitivity at the door. Chances are, if they are willing to talk with you, their intent is not to hurt you further, but to be open and honest with you.

Get Curious and Stay Interested

Cut out all distractions so that you can be fully present with the other individual. Show curiosity and interest, and let the opposing party know that you genuinely want their perspective. This reinforces the idea that you want to solve the problem, not just that you are doing it because of your own selfish needs. Set all expectations aside, throw judgment out the window, and make sure that you're willing to listen to their feelings and opinions.

End With a Solution or Purpose

Once you have engaged in the conversation and listened to each other's perspectives, summarize where the issue currently stands. Summarize the main points of view and any areas of disagreement and common ground. If there has been a resolution to the argument, confirm what it is. If there has not been a resolution, commit to discussing it again when you have had a chance to consider what you talked about.

Chapter Summary

Verbal communication is the foundation for resolving conflict. Verbal communication requires skill and practice. In this chapter, you learned:

- What verbal communication is.

- How dialogue is used.

- What effective speaking is.

- The different skills you need to send the right message.

- What active listening skills are.

- What a difficult conversation is.

- How to manage challenging conversations.

In the next chapter, you will learn about non-verbal communication and why it's vital to successful conflict resolution. You will learn about body language, how to read someone else's body language and how to diffuse situations using non-verbal communication.

CHAPTER FOUR

Conflict Resolution Technique 02 - Mastering the Power of Conversation Through Non-Verbal Communication

Non-verbal communication is a way to express yourself that does not involve words. The truth is that we use non-verbal communication every time we talk, and every time we walk into a room. We use non-verbal communication as a way to communicate with others. There are many components to non-verbal communication. It's the way you move, listen, look, stand, present yourself and react. When you become aware of your body language you can learn how to emphasize the right message. What your body language says can influence the outcome of your conversations and disputes. For example, did you know that the space you put between you and other people is a non-verbal communication tactic? Or that your emotions play a role in the movements you make and the expressions on your face? Did you know that to improve non-verbal communication, you must become very aware of yourself and others?

Conflict can arise when you use negative body language or when verbal and non-verbal cues are sending opposite signals. For example, if your voice is calm and quiet, but your arms are crossed and you don't make eye contact, this can seem condescending or rude. However, when you use open, non-threatening body language and face someone while making eye contact, it shows that you are treating them as an equal and are willing to listen to what is being said. A few examples of non-verbal communication are discussed below.

Facial Expressions

Most of us are familiar with the use of facial expressions to express ourselves. A wink is a sign of flirtation or a shared secret, a smile is a sign of friendliness or approval, a raised eyebrow is a sign of sarcasm or lack of understanding, a scrunched forehead represents a person deep in thought or concerned about something, etc. You can generally tell how a person feels or what their mood is simply by looking at their faces. Did you know that facial expressions are a universal language? When you are sad, tears may form, or a frown may be present. A smile is a facial expression that represents happiness. Anger is displayed with furrowed brows, intense stares, clenched teeth, and pursed lips. These facial expressions are the same in every country across the planet.

Movement and Posture

Mirroring someone's posture or gestures is usually a sign that there is a connection forming. It is a way to make the other person more comfortable with you. What our movements and posture say about our moods and the way we carry ourselves says a lot. For example, if you're walking with a straight posture and your head and eyes are looking straight ahead, it implies that you are a confident person on a mission. If you were walking with a slouch, eyes to the ground and your pace is slow, you may not seem confident or you may seem upset. That being said, everyone has their own style of movement, so it's unfair to say that body language is always consistent with a certain mood. Some people move around a lot, which can be a sign of anxiety for you. However, just because these ways of acting may indicate anxiety or low confidence to you, it doesn't necessarily mean that that individual lacks self-esteem or is anxious.

Gestures

Facial expressions are universal, but gestures, such as hand signals are not. What thumbs up means in one part of the world may not mean the same thing somewhere else in the world. Gestures include waving, pointing, shaking your fists, talking with your hands (waving them in the air, or using your fingers as a form of sign language to get your verbal point across). People from similar cultural backgrounds or regions usually share common gestures and are able to communicate partially using them.

Eye Contact

Looking directly into the eyes of someone else is a prominent characteristic of friendly communication. You will make eye contact with your boss if you are having a serious discussion. You would look at your friend in the eyes if you are trying to resolve a dispute or debate. There are different ways to look at people that can make you seem friendly, serious, angry, or sad. The way you look at someone can send different types of messages. For example, you wouldn't look at your boss the same way you would look at your husband or wife. Eye contact can represent interest, hostility or affection depending on how it is used.

Touch

A light touch on the cheek represents interest or affection. A nudge after a joke suggests a shared experience and closer bonds. A firm grip on the arm, leg, or other parts of the body suggest hostility, control or fear. As you can see, communication through touch can send many messages. How would you interpret a weak or overly strong handshake? How does a close and tight hug make you feel? Touch isn't just about the physical contact you get from someone; it is also about the emotion it creates for you. For example, if you receive a hug from a family member, you are going to feel happy and warm, whereas if you received a hug from someone you are in conflict with, you might not be comfortable.

Personal Space

Personal space, otherwise known as proximity, is the distance between individuals or groups. The space between people can influence our sense of comfort or safety. For example, if you are standing in line at a grocery store and you can feel the person behind you literally breathing down your neck, what would you do? How would you feel, and why? In a similar scenario, would it be okay if the person standing that close to you was a spouse or a best friend?

The spaces between people create the boundary of our comfort zone. For example, if you are the type of person that likes your own space around you, then you will have a limit on how close even your friends can be to you. You may not like hugging people to say hello. If you are more of a physical, touchy person, then less space is no concern to you. You may hug or shake hands with everyone. People feel different about the proximity they have to other people. Misunderstanding how much space people need between them can lead to conflict or make conflict resolution more difficult.

Non-verbal communication can go wrong very quickly. The way you carry yourself, the way others see you, your sense of presence, your actions, and your expressions all speak to others without using words. If you are good at poker, you would be good at hiding your body language. If you are poor at non-verbal communication skills or are unable to control them, someone playing poker with you might be able to call your bluff quickly, resulting in a loss for you. When non-verbal communication goes wrong, it's often because there are mixed signals. The individual is unaware of the messages they are sending, which makes the opposing party's attempt to interpret body language unsuccessful. Here's an example: Person A and person B just met a week ago and they are on a coffee date. Person A has a nervous twitch and finds it difficult to keep eye contact. Person B sits up straight and holds a confident pose which they expect person A to have as well. During the whole date, person A isn't nervous, and the conversation flows nicely, but their body language is not attentive. Person B interprets this non-verbal communication as disrespectful and points it out to person A. This results in a dispute over the fact that person B doesn't feel like person A was interested or listening. Person A tries to apologize but is still unaware of their body language and doesn't look at person B while apologizing so person B doesn't feel the apology was genuine and becomes offended. The coffee date ends in a disagreement.

The problem here was that person A was unaware of how their behavior was perceived, and person B interpreted the body language of person A incorrectly. Person A has always behaved that way so they felt no wrongdoing on their part. However, because person B doesn't know person A very well, they received mixed signals which upset them. Non-verbal communication can go very wrong so it is important we understand it, and how it can contribute to conflict. Learn appropriate and effective ways of communicating non-verbally. This will help to send the message you want to convey.

Signs That Conflict is on the Rise

Conflict can happen in any situation and it can happen when you are least expecting it. The goal is to figure out ways to resolve it or diffuse it before it begins. Most people are unaware of the signs that dispute is about to happen. You must know what to look for. Read your own body language and that of others. Most of the time you can read the signs of negative feelings just by watching for specific non-verbal cues. Some symptoms include finger or foot tapping, squeezing the temples, rubbing the forehead or back of the neck, furrowed brows, or tense postures. If you catch yourself feeling heated or recognize that your patience is thinning, it might be time to take a personal break to collect yourself before an argument happens. Some people might not even know that you are bothered so this a good time to calm down. If you notice the person you are with is using those non-verbal cues, you can use that knowledge to diffuse the situation.

Be sure to interpret non-verbal cues correctly. For example, tapping of the foot or fingers is often a sign of anxiety, not just irritation. The same goes for irregular breathing. Often, we find ourselves puffing out a hot breath when we become heated or frustrated, so it may seem like someone is angry if they are doing the same. Really, it could just be that they are short of breath or anxious. Look at various expressions of their body language and derive a conclusion. If brows are furrowed, the forehead is wrinkled, and their facial expression resembles disgust or disappointment, it is a sign that an argument may be about to break out. Along with anxiety or other emotional signals, you can tell if a person is angry by their sudden movements. If someone is pacing, they might be deep in thought, or they might be mad. So, if there are many signals communicated with body language, and they may not all have the same meanings to different people, how do you tell if someone is angry or not? If you aren't sure, ask them.

Imagine you are watching your neighbors argue in their front yard. In this example, we will use the woman as the one who is angry with the man. You cannot hear what's going on, but you see her arms flail up in the air, her head is shaking from side to side, her face is flushed, and she keeps moving her feet as if ants are biting at them. The man is standing very still and then tries to leave by turning his back on her. This is when you notice her grab his arm firmly and appear to shout something. You clearly see that her eyes are like daggers, and her teeth are firmly clenched. The man then turns to face her and tries to give her a hug, but she turns away by whipping her whole body around and marching to the front door of their house. The man leaves. In this example, you recognize the body language used by the woman as frustration and anger, but why? How did you know they were having a fight? Throughout the entire episode, her facial expressions and body movements were angry and agitated. She was scowling, her arms flailed, she was yelling, she would not accept his hug. These are all clear signs of anger or frustration.

In this specific example, the couple is unable to resolve the conflict at that time. Both parties walk away, which is a very clear body language. Before a conflict escalates to that point, minimize negative body language to keep a conversation on track. Some things that can cause conflict to happen or escalate are as follows:

- **Being distracted:** During the conversation, distractions can turn another person off and will send the message that you don't care to hear what they need to say.

- **Not making eye contact:** Lack of eye-contact shows that you are not focused on the speaker. If eye-contact is a problem for you, state this, and use other forms of communicating to show that you are there to listen.

- **Playing on your phone or digital device:** Even if you think you are listening with your full attention, you are not. When you use devices and phones during a conversation you are only partially listening to the speaker since your eyes are looking at your phone. You can't fully understand how the person is feeling or what their message conveys if you aren't listening fully and observing their body language.

- **Seeming off in space or not responding:** This body language shows a lack of respect and the individual will feel there is no point in having a conversation since you don't seem to be really listening. Responding to the other person shows you are listening and thinking about what they have said.

- **Talking too fast or too quiet:** Whether we realize it or not, talking too fast or too quiet can upset people because they have to try too hard to understand, and it can be a sign of being untrustworthy. It can be hard to follow and lead to misunderstandings or frustration.

- **Invading personal space:** Personal space defines our level of comfort around others. It may be in place due to our morals, boundaries and values or because of our personal experiences. Once our space has been invaded, it feels as though the opposing party isn't respecting us, and we may feel cornered or attacked. We may be so distracted by the lack of personal space that we can't concentrate on the dialogue. We may act defensively, guard ourselves or act impulsively.

- **Closed body language:** In times of conflict, you may use closed-body language posture if you are defending yourself because there is a safety issue. However, when you are just conversing, a closed way of presenting yourself implies that you are unapproachable, grumpy or disinterested.

Displaying positive body language shows that you care and are paying attention. Next time you are talking with someone, think about your body language and then try to picture them using the same body language. How would you feel? What would you think? Use body language to help convey your message, to understand the signals you put out when you act in certain ways, and to evaluate the moods of others. If you want to send the message that you are angry and frustrated, then use the body language that sends that message. If you want to portray that you are happy, then you must use open, positive non-verbal tools that communicate that message.

Conflict Diffusion Techniques

Effective conflict resolution using non-verbal communication involves seeing others, being seen, and/or interacting face-to-face with others. Using non-verbal skills can stop conflict from escalating further. Most conflicts happen in the workplace or the home. This can impact our most important professional or intimate relationships. For the examples in this section, let's consider work-related and relationship scenarios. Here are ways to use non-verbal tools to diffuse conflict before it escalates:

- Take a personal moment.

  ○ Count to ten, twenty, thirty, etc. until you have calmed down.

  ○ Inhale deeply through your nose and exhale through your mouth letting all the air escape your lungs.

  ○ Clear your head, then return to the conversation or point of conflict.

- Be aware. Observe and notice everything.

  ○ What are you feeling?

  ○ What kind of body language are you using?

  ○ How is the other person acting?

  ○ What is the speaker expressing with their body language?

  ○ How much space is between you and them?

- Keep a calm composure.

  ○ Maintain eye-contact but try not to glare at the other person.

  ○ Breathe at a steady, easy pace.

  ○ Keep your facial expressions open, welcoming, or expressionless.

  ○ Appear willing to listen and stay empathetic.

  ○ Stand or sit straight.

  ○ Try not to fidget or become distracted by your surroundings.

- Listen.

  ○ Listen attentively.

- ○ Lean forward a little so they know you are paying attention.
- ○ Nod your head periodically to show that you heard and understand.
- ○ If you are unsure, use a questioning look to convey your confusion.

Most of the time, when we keep a calm composure and listen effectively, we can diffuse a conflict before it begins. In doing this, you must be completely aware of your own emotions, thoughts, and behaviors so that you can display positive responses. Show empathy throughout the conversation and make sure that you also feel safe. Remain calm and open even when the opposing party seems frustrated or hostile. Your positive non-verbal communication will have a calming, reassuring effect on others. If their body language continues to escalate in a negative direction, sometimes it is best to end the conversation and walk away. This is especially true if you are unsure about your safety.

Learning the POP Method

POP is an acronym for Person, Object and Place. This method is used mainly in the workplace or when a conflict has the potential for violence. Sometimes, resolving conflict is not an option, so that is why we must learn about POP to protect ourselves from danger. Have you ever felt heightened nervousness or anxiety? You may shake, can't think or feel like running. You may have difficulty breathing or feel nauseous. It's almost as if you forget everything, and all you know is the desire to survive. In a state of anxiousness or overwhelming emotions, your body may have a fight-or-flight response.

Person relates to the party you are in conflict with. The first part of the POP model requires you to take into account the details about who you are in conflict with. Notice their height, weight, ethnicity, age, gender, body type, etc. Observe the facts objectively without judgment. Just because someone may look intense, intimidating, and dangerous, doesn't mean that they will act threatening. Similarly, someone who is small or diminutive may be more dangerous than they look. Try to take note of the deeper aspects of their personality and behavior. What is their temperament, characteristics, mental or emotional state, etc.? Are they displaying aggressive tendencies? How vulnerable are they?

Object refers to what items are in the room and accessible to you and the person you are in conflict with. Are there weapons present? Are there pointy or heavy objects close to you or the individual that can be used as a weapon or in defense? If you are unsure and there are no visible signs of a weapon present, do not assume that there isn't one. For your safety, it's best to believe the person is equipped to harm you if the conflict escalates physically. Keep in mind that anything can be used as a weapon, including a phone book, a bottle, a fork, etc.

Place is where you are located. What environment are you in? This includes places like bars, outside, in your own home, at a friend's house, in the workplace, etc. Observing your environment plays a significant role in guessing what could happen in the heat of the moment. For example, if you are at work, it's less likely someone will make a scene,

59

whereas if you are alone with them things could turn heated or violent. Are you somewhere you are familiar with? Do you know all the exit routes? Notice whether it's night or day, rain, or shine, cold or warm because this might impact why the person is in a moody or angry state.

When in doubt, trust your gut feeling. If someone is using body language that you find threatening find a way to get out quickly. The most important rule in being safe is always to be aware of yourself, the other person, and what is around you.

Learning the SAFER Method

The acronym for **SAFER** means - Step back, assess threat, Find help, Evaluate options, Respond. This method can be used anywhere, including the workplace, at home or in public places. When someone's body language is threatening to you, these tools can help you respond to danger.

Step back: This means to stop, look, listen, and remain calm. Acting impulsively may escalate the danger and prevent us from observing crucial facts. When we act irrationally, we don't think clearly and cannot make wise decisions based on the facts of the situation.

Assess threat: From your lesson about POP, you know how to assess the situation for danger. Look at the person, read their body language, assume there are weapons present, and evaluate your environment for weapons or defensive tools.

Find help: Look for an escape route or means of rescue. It may be a door or window, a means of transportation or communication, or another person. Know who is around you and how far. If you are at home, is your neighbor home? How far away is your phone? If you are at work, where is the next available person located? If it seems that there is no help, remain calm and keep thinking and observing.

Evaluate options: After you have gone through the options available for finding help, decide which is your best route to safety. Is conversation an option for settling the angry party, or do you need to enlist the help of someone else? Do you need to find a way out?

Respond: After you have considered all your options, the final step is to follow through with what you have decided. Be prepared for things to change and make sure that you have a plan B and even a plan C if necessary.

Chapter Summary

It may take time, patience, and practice to fully understand how non-verbal communication can help us diffuse conflict. Mastering non-verbal communication will make it easier for you to read people's behaviors before, during, and after conflict. It will also help you to manage your own body language to ensure you portray the right message and do not contribute to misunderstandings.

In this chapter, you learned:

- What non-verbal communication is and why it's important.

- How to recognize signs of conflict before it happens.

- How to diffuse a situation before it escalates.

- The POP safety measure.

- The SAFER safety measures.

In the next chapter, you will learn about emotions, how they contribute to conflict, and how to manage yours during a conflict situation.

CHAPTER FIVE

Conflict Resolution Technique 03 - Managing Emotions

When it comes to emotions and conflict, the fact is that we become so engaged in conversation that we may become unaware of how we are feeling in the moment. This happens because when we are in a friendly and approachable environment, we don't need to be in tune with our emotions as much. We get so comfortable that we may not notice a conflict arising. Perhaps a trigger word might have been said, a disruptive statement might have been made, or a certain vibe or body language might suddenly catch you or the other person off guard. As conflict starts to build, the heart rate quickens, breathing becomes short, thoughts go a mile a minute, etc. All of this heightened emotion increases, and before you know it, you say things you don't mean, you do things out of emotional impulse, and you become angry, depressed, anxious, etc.

So, how do you stop your emotions from spiraling out of control? How do you begin to notice the signs that you or those around you are becoming emotional? You have to be aware of your emotional state before and during the conflict. You must commit to observing the behaviors of yourself and others. You must learn self-awareness strategies and be mindful in almost every moment so that you can manage your emotions.

Developing Self-Awareness

Self-awareness is the ability to recognize and notice your own thoughts, feelings, character, motives, and desires as they happen. A person who has the keen ability to be self-aware means that they notice when their heart quickens or when their body language or tone changes. The self-aware take the time to evaluate themselves in every situation. Self-awareness requires you to be in tune with yourself and your personality and to understand your typical behaviors. You must know your strengths, weaknesses, beliefs and what makes you who you are. Self-awareness isn't just about yourself, though. It's also about seeing and understanding how others perceive you and how to tell when you have done something to upset someone else. It's about knowing what triggers you and being aware enough to understand other people and how they are feeling. It may be you or the environment, or they might be triggering themselves. Developing self-awareness is crucial to understanding and noticing things before they happen. This plays a significant role in resolving or diffusing conflict. Here are things you can do to start working on your self-awareness right now:

Take a Step Back and Observe Yourself

Sometimes we get so caught up in our own lives that we forget to take a step back to re-evaluate ourselves periodically. If you take the time to look at yourself objectively, you can define which aspects of yourself you don't like and work on changing them. Getting to know yourself in this way is incredibly rewarding. It might include the following actions:

- Think of things you are proud of yourself for.

- Identify your strengths and weaknesses.

- Capitalize on your strengths.

- Work on your weaknesses.

- Reward yourself often.

- Practice self-discipline often.

- Think about what makes you truly happy.

- Be honest with yourself.

Keeping a Journal

Journaling is proven to benefit our lives in many ways. You can write about anything in your journal. A few examples are:

- Your life.

- Your fears and concerns.

- Your goals and aspirations.

- Your strengths and weaknesses.

- Your thoughts.

- Your dreams.

- Notes about other people.

- Your meditation techniques (what works, what doesn't).

- Your fitness goals and accomplishments.

- A dietary record.

The possibilities are endless. Journaling is about writing what's on your mind so that you can vent, look at it from a different perspective, and gain insight into yourself. Sometimes it's used as a way to let go of thoughts by writing them down so that you can move on to other thoughts. It's a self-reflection technique and it has been proven to boost moods and motivate you to figure out what you want in your life.

Practice Self-Reflection

At the start of every day, wake up and ask yourself what you want from the day. What do you want to accomplish? How do you want to live today? At the end of every day, ask yourself if you accomplished what you set out to do today. Ask yourself if there is anything you would do differently. Reflect on the highs and lows of the day and define how you can do better tomorrow. These questions are not about self-judgment but about opening your mind to notice and understand your thoughts and behaviors. Self-awareness and self-reflection help you know yourself which leads to knowing where you want to go in life, and makes it more likely for you to get there.

Practice Mindfulness

Mindfulness is the practice of being one with yourself in this present moment. Put aside your thoughts, feelings, beliefs, and just be here with yourself. For example, when you are drinking a nice warm cup of tea, look at it as if you have never seen it before. You are tasting the tea for the first time. You are holding a hot cup for the first time. You are noticing the different colors on your mug for the first time. Mindfulness is practicing feeling and experiencing the moment you are in right now to its fullest. Right now, you are reading a section on self-awareness because you want to learn how to resolve conflict quickly and efficiently. So, at this very moment, nothing else matters. Don't think about what's happening outside or what someone else is doing. All that matters is right now, and the rest of the world can wait. Tada! You just completed a short moment of being completely mindful. Being mindful is not:

- Judging yourself.

- Questioning yourself or anything around you.

- Thinking about one thing then letting your mind drift to another thing.

Your first few times at practicing mindfulness might be challenging, and you will get distracted. When that happens, bring yourself back to the moment and focus again on what you are experiencing at that time.

Ask for Feedback

Knowing what others think of you but not taking it personally can help you identify what you need to work on. You can ask your most trusted friend about how you really are or how you appear to others, and if you don't like the answer you can work on changing it. If you do like the answer, then congratulate yourself for being perceived exactly how you want to be. Use self-awareness when you want to fix a behavior and you are trying to figure out when that side of you comes out. Learning to identify a trigger, emotion or setback in the moment it happens can sometimes only be achieved by getting feedback from others you trust.

Self-awareness happens when we are open to constructive criticism but do not judge ourselves and others. It is okay if you lack confidence or if you question yourself daily. Using strategies for learning self-awareness can also help to develop self-esteem.

Dealing With Anger During Conflict

A situation often results in conflict when someone feels that something is unfair and they get angry. We all have different personalities, different beliefs, and different ways of doing things. No two people are the same and though you can never be sure how someone will react, anger is a common emotion that people express during conflict. Many relationships end because individuals cannot manage anger during conflict. In extreme cases, this can lead to aggression and violence.

Some people have an angrier temperament than others or are more prone to angry outbursts or reactions. This temperament may be due to past experiences, learned behavior or inner conflict. Overcoming anger requires acceptance that there is a problem. Do you become heated out of nowhere? Does one person make you angrier than anyone else? Do certain situations regularly trigger intense emotion? Find out what your triggers are and then work at managing your anger before it contributes to conflict.

Here are a few ways you can manage anger or other intense emotions when you are in a conflict situation.

Patience

Managing anger and other emotions takes patience not just with another person, but also with yourself. Using patience as a self-awareness tool requires you to pause when you feel an intense emotion and suppress it before it contributes to a conflict. Patience is all about time; time to consider perspectives, time to allow your anger to calm down, time to stop crying, time to breathe, time to listen. Patience works with others as well. When you take the time to calmly approach a situation in an unhurried manner, others are less likely to escalate the situation, as our patient behavior has a calming effect on those around us.

Breathing

Using breathing techniques to manage intense emotions during a conflict requires that you work on staying mindful of your body. Breathe slowly and deeply and focus on the moment. The breathing strategy works to soothe almost all intense emotions. When you become irate, hysterical, or have a panic attack, you will notice your breath shortens, or you may hyperventilate or hold your breath. This is the time to take a moment to yourself to just breathe. The best way to breathe out your frustration is by deep breathing. There are a few ways to do deep breathing. Here is one method of deep breathing:

1. If you are able to, go somewhere quiet where you can be alone.

2. You can do this exercise sitting, standing, or lying down.

3. Some people find it helpful to put one hand on the stomach and one hand on the chest to help you focus.

4. This exercise is most commonly done with the eyes closed, but it can also be done with the eyes focused on something calming or pretty.

5. Breathe in through your nose for a count of 3-5 seconds, allowing your belly to rise, then your chest to rise.

6. Hold your breath for 3 seconds.

7. Release your breath slowly through your mouth for a count of 3-5 seconds.

8. Repeat the breathing pattern, concentrating on filling your belly, then your chest, then exhaling fully but slowly.

9. Repeat the breathing exercise until you feel your body and mind settle and calm. Some people do up to 10 repetitions several times a day as part of their regular health routine!

10. End your breathing session by opening your eyes and slowly returning your breath back to normal.

11. Get up carefully and slowly.

Some people also do a variation where they only allow their bellies to rise and fall or just their chest. Try all of them, and find out what works best for you.

If you are trying to breathe discreetly during a conflict, simply put your hands in a comfortable position and breathe deeply, quietly, and slowly. Even doing it once or twice can be enough to have a calming effect.

Walk Away

Sometimes, a dispute can get out of hand, and that's when hurtful words and actions can occur. Before this happens, walk away from whatever is upsetting or angering you. If it's a person, let them know you cannot engage any further and that you need a break. Tell them that you are walking away to clear your head, not because you are unwilling to resolve the conflict. Sometimes, they might call after you as you walk away, but in some situations, this is your only option. Upon walking away, distract your mind from what is bothering you. Some things you can do are:

- Go for a light jog.

- Take a walk in the park or around the block.

- Work on a project you have in progress.

- Pick up a hobby.

- Watch a show, listen to music or an audiobook.

- Read a book, eBook, magazine or blog.

- Call a friend or family member to see how they are.

- Deep breathing.

This might seem like an obvious technique, or you might think that it isn't really a technique at all. When our emotions are heightened, we often don't think before we act or we say things to escalate the conflict further. Have you ever been in a disagreement where you get interrupted, or nothing you say seems to be working? Now voices are raised, body language is negative, facial expressions are hostile or sad, and whatever pops into your head flies out of your mouth before you can take it back. Patience and breathing should be used before a dispute escalates, but if you need to, let the opposing party know that you need to walk away and take some time to think before responding so that you don't say the wrong thing.

Laugh a Little

Okay, so you are probably wondering if humor should be used but you are concerned about using it at the right time and place, right? Sometimes conflicts escalate because we are taking things too seriously, or don't take the time to laugh at ourselves and try to make light of a situation. Humor can be effective to redirect anger and move toward resolution. Make sure the humor is not an insult to either party. For example, if you and your partner are in the middle of a huge argument, instead of having things escalate even further, you could make a humorous statement such as, "geez, if this gets any more heated, we might just have to get someone to hose us down." This should result in both of you laughing with each other. Make sure you are laughing *with* one another, not *at* one another. Hopefully, it will lighten the situation.

As long as you are genuine, and make sure there is no sarcasm or condescending attitude, humor may get you to a more positive place.

Positive Self-Talk

Often we listen too much to our inner critic or the opinions of others, and this makes us question our identity or point of view. When in a difficult conversation, if someone has insulted you or insists you are wrong, instead of reacting negatively and escalating the conflict, use positive self-talk to manage your emotions. You can say to yourself:

- I believe in myself.

- Breathe (your name) it's okay, this isn't going to last forever.

- I am okay, I am fully capable of handling myself appropriately.

- They are mad, and they don't mean what they are saying.

- I am confident about my point of view.

- I will not let their words hurt me or impact my self-esteem.

- I am not going to react in anger.

Positive self-talk is about calming yourself down, supporting yourself and believing in your position. Do not accept the negativity directed at you.

Forgiveness

Forgiveness can be hard. It requires you to let go of your anger and no longer harbor resentment. You may be upset with another person, or even with yourself. It could be because someone did something bad to you or someone you love. It could be because you disagree about something that was done without asking your permission or opinion. Some things are easier to forgive than others. Forgiveness isn't always about forgiving another person, but about forgiving yourself for contributing to the conflicts in your life, or for something bad that you did. Holding onto anger, frustration or hatred means that you have less space in your mind and heart for the happy and positive things in life.

Be More Accommodating and Less Prideful

Often, pride clouds our vision. We feel superior, or we compete to win an argument because it's in our nature. If your pride doesn't allow you to back down and accommodate the needs of others, then you will likely have a lot of conflict in your life. You may have been taught to do unto others as they have done to you. But why must you conform to these beliefs and aim to hurt someone else? Just because someone insults you or disagrees with you doesn't mean you have to be angry or retaliate. When you have been in a heated disagreement, have you walked away regretting something that you said or did? If you answered yes, it's because pride has gotten in the way. Let go of your inflated ego, and stay accommodating while practicing assertiveness and boundary control.

These techniques are presented to give you options when you are in a conflict situation. No one strategy or method works for every person. You can try different tactics, examine the outcomes, and decide which tools work best for you in various situations. Only you know what works best for you, so try something for a little while, and if it doesn't work, try something else. You may have to use a combination of strategies to manage your own heightened emotions when in a conflict.

Chapter Summary

Perhaps the most important lesson that you have learned during this chapter is that by managing our emotions we have a better chance of resolving conflict. Managing our emotions by developing self-awareness and dealing with emotions such as anger can help us diffuse a conflict before it escalates.

In this chapter, you learned:

- How to build self-awareness.

- Techniques to manage heightened emotions before they escalate.

- How to let go of anger during conflict.

- In the next chapter, you will learn about how to use persuasion and negotiation to change the minds of those around you.

CHAPTER SIX

Conflict Resolution Technique 04 - Changing Minds through Persuasion and Negotiation

Technique number four in conflict resolution is about how to change people's minds, including your own, through perspective, persuasion, and negotiation. We often try to solve a dispute the same way we settled our previous conflict, yet the current situation may be different from the previous experience. What most people don't realize is that there is no "one size fits all" solution to resolving conflict.

The reason it is important to understand the perspective of yourself and others is so you can empathize with how a conflict appears to someone besides you. Once you understand what is happening, you can become better at persuading others to see your side of things. As you have learned in the previous chapters, reacting emotionally or being verbally and non-verbally aggressive limits the options for resolving conflict. Understanding someone else's perspective tells you how the person thinks and why they respond the way they do. During a conflict, some people don't consider another's perspectives because they are prideful or want to win an argument rather than resolving the conflict to the mutual benefit of both parties. If the goal is to come to an agreement or compromise, then sacrifices can be made to find middle ground and resolution. If you respond to a conflict in a competitive or prideful way because you want to "win" the argument, the outcome may be that you lose your job, your friend, or your spouse as a result.

Adopting the perspective of someone else for the purpose of understanding their position can increase our chance to persuade others and negotiate a resolution. The benefits of understanding and adopting the perspectives of others are:

- Gaining more information about the situation.

- Learning more about yourself and another individual.

- Enabling you to choose effective verbal and non-verbal strategies.

- Promoting listening skills.

- Increasing the chances for healthy relationships.

- Helping us define who we are.

- Creating empathy.

According to Michael Carroll, an expert in neuro-linguistic programming (NLP), using what's called the triple position means that you use a combination of three different ways of looking at things in order to fully engage and understand the perspectives of a situation. The first position is to look at yourself, which you also learned about in the previous chapter about self-awareness. The second position is viewing things from the other side and using empathy and emotional intelligence to increase the chances for resolution. The third position is to look at the situation from the neutral overview perspective. Lastly, when you achieve the triple position, you are able to look at each party's perspective, as well as the whole picture to create a greater understanding of the overall situation.

First Position: Self

Think of the first position in the same way that you would think of the first-person point of view in writing. It's your perspective and personal opinion on what's happening in any type of event or situation. First position means that you are only looking at things from your own point of view and no one else's. First person perspective can be both negative and/or positive. Often, the first position is adopted by the people who are competitive, narrow-minded, and self-absorbed. You can use the first position to be in tune with yourself completely, or you can consider your own perspective while being selfishly obsessed. It can be positive when you feel your own emotions fully and can go after what you want with a clear picture of the goal in mind.

Second Position: Others

An example of someone who uses the second position is a therapist, sales associate, mediator, or judge. These people must clearly understand the perspective of others in order to do their job. These types of people have significant negotiation skills and can understand another person's way of thinking. Second position is much like explaining or viewing something from the second-person point of view in a story. For example, in storytelling, the writer is using "you/he/she/they/them" statements and telling the story in a way that speaks directly to the audience. Second person point of view is a general way of speaking rather than being about an individual's personal perspective of their experience. Adopting the second position in conflict resolution requires you to be empathetic and understanding when it comes to another's thoughts and feelings.

Third Position: Observer

Telling a story from the third person point of view explains every aspect of the story. This is also called narrative style. You aren't writing from the perspective of one of the characters. Instead, you are describing the whole picture, such as he felt XXX, she said XXX. It's the explanation of what's happening to every character in a story. Third position is the last position in the triple perception experience where you, as an individual, can take a step back and view the scene as a whole. Think of it as if you have taken a step outside of yourself. You are no longer looking at your own emotions or feeling empathy for someone else's perspective or thoughts. Instead, you have taken a complete step out of the situation and are now looking at it as an outsider - the third person. This position is helpful when you want to reflect on everyone's behavior or when you want to evaluate a situation objectively, non-judgmentally and non-emotionally.

The Combination: Triple Position

In a triple position perspective, you successfully combine all these positions and use them to deal with conflict effectively. Typically, a dispute will arise if each party in the conflict is stuck in first position. Ultimately it is not our fault if we view things from the first position because we are all unique and individualistic and often focused on our own needs, so it only makes sense that we view things from the first position. When you actively build upon your empathy skills, you are practicing the second position. As you practice observation of the overall situation, you are mastering the third position. Now you can move into the triple position by using the positions at the same time, which is ultimately the most helpful in resolving conflicts. These skills can be used before, during, and after a dispute has taken place.

Perspective is about using your self-awareness, social skills, leadership abilities, and observation abilities to fully understand a situation and redefine it altogether. Using the triple position tool promotes success in resolving conflict. When reading the rest of this chapter, keep in mind the power of perspective using the triple position method.

What is Persuasion? What is Negotiation?

Conflict resolution requires that we learn how to change the minds of others through persuasion and negotiation. As much as persuasion and negotiation may seem alike, they have very distinct differences. Basically, the fundamental difference between persuasion and negotiation is that persuasion is the art of informing someone such that they change their mind and take your side, and negotiation is more like bargaining or trading concessions until both people agree on what will be the final agreed position. Fundamental to both persuasion and negotiation is understanding what is the primary interest of all parties involved.

Persuasion

Persuasion is the ability to get someone to do something by asking, proving your point, or conversing with the intent that they adopt a different way of thinking. Persuasion is a form of communication which may include informing, convincing, entertaining, and narrating. It is well known that persuasion can be a manipulative tactic, but if used correctly with the right motive, persuasive techniques don't have to have devious intent. To be persuasive, you must first explain your situation or reasoning, then explain all the benefits of your position. Persuasive tactics include:

- Debating.

- Informing.

- Convincing.

- Influencing.

- Finding commonality.

Negotiation

Negotiation means to reach an agreement among all parties, and it is well known as a conflict resolution strategy. The outcome of a negotiation is usually that neither party gets exactly what they asked for, but both will get aspects of what they want. This is done by mutually agreeing about what concessions are possible for either side. During a negotiation, fairness, mutual understanding, and benefit, and maintaining trust and closeness are essential factors to consider. Negotiation uses tools such as:

- **Questioning:** Ask the other party questions to obtain an understanding of the facts or the perspective and needs of others.

- **Exploring:** Find out the needs of all parties and explain them to each other. Use the answers to the questions to inspire conversation.

- **Motivation:** Understand what motivates the parties to argue or insist on their position. Are they driven by morality, finances, or other specific issues?

- **Priorities:** What are the things that each party wants the most, and what will each party give up to resolve the conflict?

How Do You Choose?

In deciding which tactic or technique to use when trying to change someone's mind or perspective, you must decide if the primary goal is an outcome that will benefit all parties in the conflict. Most people will choose persuasion over negotiation because their primary purpose is to convince someone to take on their point of view. They may not really understand or even care about the needs of the other person. Other people will choose negotiation when their goal is to find common ground. Most people resort to persuasion tactics because we primarily take the first position perspective, and it is hard to negotiate with someone if we only consider our own needs. Negotiation can only become possible when we use the second position. However, it is not a rule that you only use one or the other. When persuasion is combined with negotiation, you may find that the end result is a better outcome than if you were to choose just one approach to changing someone's mind.

How to Resolve Conflict Through Persuasion and Negotiation

This section of the chapter will help you identify persuasion strategies and negotiation strategies so that you can use both of them to resolve conflict. When you are focusing on being persuasive, you must take emotions into consideration and adopt emotional intelligence to gain insight on how to influence your audience. When you focus on negotiation, you must take empathy and reading someone's body language into account before proposing your compromise.

Using Positive Persuasion Techniques to Resolve Conflict

Approaching conflict with a positive attitude increases the chance of an amicable resolution. There are many positive persuasion techniques you can use. We will discuss five of them below: positive reinforcement, respect, opportunism, acknowledgment, and success.

1. Positive reinforcement

Positive reinforcement strategy is used in child development. It's where you ignore bad or challenging behaviors and enforce positive behaviors. Rather than paying attention to temper tantrums and aggressiveness, you would instead make every good thing a child does a big deal. For example, if a child paints a pretty picture or counts to ten on their own, you would clap and say, "Wow, good job." If they have an angry outburst, you might ignore them instead of yelling.

Positive reinforcement as a persuasive tactic requires you to praise the actions of the other person in order to encourage them to act in a manner that is favorable to you. If you foresee a potential conflict, you might thank them for previous consideration they have given you. For example, if you are trying to persuade a friend to help you with your truck, you might start by thanking them again for the last time they helped you.

2. Respect

This strategy involves showing genuine consideration of the assets or accomplishments of the other person. You can remind them of their best qualities in order to help them imagine themselves again doing something generous or helpful. When you want to show that you respect and believe in someone, provide proof by explaining why. Then paint a picture about how they are the only ones who can truly help you. This will encourage them to consider doing it.

3. Opportunism

Seek opportunities to get what you need or want by understanding the habits and preferences of the other person. For example, if you need to borrow money and know that a generous colleague likes to go for coffee, you would arrange to run into them at their preferred coffee shop, have coffee with them, and then persuade them to lend you money.

4. Acknowledgment

Much like the two previous strategies, using acknowledgment in persuasion means to use someone's accomplishments to help you get what want. In a conflict scenario such as a dispute with a coworker who involves themselves in your personal business too much, you may need to create a positive situation before you are comfortable talking to them about the issue. You might tell them how much their skills contributed to the success of a recent project. Then you might tell them you really enjoyed working with them but that you're very private about your personal life, so you would rather just talk about work.

5. Success

If you come across someone who has a competitive nature, then you can use this in a positive way to resolve conflict with them. For most competitive people, success is their main goal in life. You can explain ways in which you are successful, and how aligning with you would be a benefit to them. This will help to persuade this individual that it would be better to stay friends with you than to stay in a dispute with you.

These strategies might seem manipulative, but consider your intentions behind the persuasion. If your motive is to get the help that benefits you both, this will lead to a positive outcome. On the other hand, if your intentions are selfish, you will seem ingenuine and likely have little success resolving the conflict. Always think of the other person's needs before you start using persuasion and negotiation tactics.

Using Negotiation Techniques to Resolve Conflict

Negotiation techniques are easier than persuasion techniques because it's easier to compromise than to sway someone completely to your side. The art of finding a middle ground, compromise and gaining mutual benefit is at the heart of negotiation. Persuasion can be used in conversation before resorting to negotiation, or you can dive straight into negotiating. If you dive right in, it might seem as if you are being aggressive and only bringing up the conversation to get something out of it. On the other hand, when you explain what you see as the conflict and ask if you can discuss a resolution in the form of compromise, you are more likely to succeed in your negotiation. Three effective negotiation tactics are:

1. Take the interests and values of each party into account.

When resolving conflict using this tactic, make sure that you are separating your own beliefs from those of the other party. Identify what their values are so that you can problem-solve around them. The opposing party will trust you more if you first let them know you were listening to their point of view and taking their values into account. Make it clear that just because you are in conflict doesn't mean that you are trying to take away what's important to them. Put everything else aside and focus on the problem at hand.

2. Develop your verbal and non-verbal communication strategy before approaching the other party.

Practicing what you want to say and how you present yourself before engaging with the other party contributes substantially to resolving a conflict. This will help you to confidently deliver your message, and make you more resilient to the reactions of the other person. You don't have to memorize every word and posture that you will use. Make a list of your main points, and practice different ways of saying them, taking the time to consider how each sound, and how it might be interpreted by the other person. While you are practicing also try out different ways to stand or sit while delivering the information. Make sure that your posture and hand gestures are calm and non-threatening.

3. Consider the common ground you have. Share this information.

Negotiation is like bargaining. It is about trading and building on what interests both parties in the conflict. Both parties should get some of what they want, and give something up to the other person. For example, if you and your sibling accidentally bought the same outfit, and you both like the piece of clothing equally, you may have a conflict if your sibling wants you to return yours. They argue that they don't want to be seen wearing the same thing as you, especially at the same time. You could start to resolve this conflict by telling your sibling that you both have great taste. Then you might propose that you will never wear it on the days that you are going to see them, and that on special holidays where both of you will be present, you will both choose a different outfit. In doing so, you both get to keep the outfit, and neither of you is seen wearing it at the same time. Point out ways you can both enjoy the outfit, and focus on the issue of being seen at the same time, rather than insisting that only one person can keep the outfit.

During a conflict or dispute, there are differences in personality, values, and opinions that can impact the outcome. Boundaries might have been crossed because of something that was said. When you address these concerns with the other party you will gain insight into the differences in your opinions, allowing you to negotiate ways around them. For example, you and your boss think that management should be handled in different ways. You think there should be more employee support but your boss feels there should be more customer support. The conflict is that there are personal differences in opinion about what should take priority. Resolving this conflict could involve identifying why you feel differently and gaining insight into both aspects of the business. Perhaps you could negotiate some improvements to both. Successful negotiating is about working together to resolve disputes so that both people win and the conflict ends. Sometimes you need to really understand your differences so that you can find common ground.

Chapter Summary

Changing the minds of others and yourself is about seeing the whole situation, coming up with a game plan, and resolving it using persuasion and negotiation strategies. This chapter was written to help you gain perspective about the triple position approach, and to assist you when using negotiation and persuasion as a conflict resolution technique. Let's recap what we've learned in this chapter. In this chapter you learned:

- The triple position.

- What persuasion is.

- What negotiation is.

- How to persuade.

- How to negotiate.

- How to resolve conflict by combining persuasion and negotiation. ·

In the next chapter, you will learn how to develop your emotional intelligence skills. This will help you succeed and resolve conflict as a great leader does.

CHAPTER SEVEN

Conflict Resolution Technique 05 - Developing Emotional Intelligence So You Can Resolve Conflict Like a Leader

Many great leaders attain success because they are great at managing and resolving conflict. How do they accomplish this? They have developed their emotional and social intelligence skills to enable them to resolve any problems that arise. You can learn how to resolve conflict like a great leader does. What else makes a great and successful leader? How does emotional intelligence contribute to success? Here are a few characteristics of great leaders:

- Leaders work on the needs of the group, and usually put others before themselves.

- Leaders are assertive, but not aggressive.

- Leaders are great conversationalists and speakers.

- Leaders learn about the people around them.

- Leaders are honest but tactful.

- Leaders know how to influence the people around them.

You don't have to be a great leader to succeed at being emotionally intelligent. Anyone can learn and use this skill. So, what is emotional intelligence exactly? It's the ability to control and regulate your own emotions while being understanding and empathetic of someone else's emotions. Everyone can learn the skills it takes to be emotionally intelligent. However, not everyone can put their skills into use when intense emotions are involved. Great leaders have this ability because they trained their minds to be emotionally stable even during conflicts. This allows them to lead large crowds and groups of people with confidence and poise. One of the main skills required for emotional intelligence is self-motivation. Sometimes that means that you aren't motivated because wealth or power is involved, but because your personal growth is. It can also mean that you are able to accomplish things without pressure from others. Let's discuss four major skills that have to do with emotional intelligence. When you use them together effectively, you can confidently state that your emotional intelligence is high. The four skills are:

1. Self-motivation.

2. Self-regulation.

3. Self-awareness.

4. Empathy.

Some people have developed these skills to a higher degree than the others. Other people have only a few or maybe none of these skills. However, if you don't have all of these skills, or are working on them still, this chapter will help you get there. Every leader is different in their own way, but what they all have in common is that they all know that conflict management requires teamwork, self-reflection, negotiation, and respect. The most effective leaders also have high emotional intelligence. By learning the different skills that lead to high emotional intelligence, you learn leadership skills that give you the ability to resolve conflict. Since we learned about self-awareness in chapter five, we will now focus on self-motivation, self-regulation, and empathy.

How to be Self-Motivating

Self-motivation is the ability to take the initiative and strive to do something without being asked or pressured by anyone else. It's the ability to see something and go after it, to fulfill your purpose, and to only be driven and motivated by yourself or the dream of the successful outcome. Some people may interpret this as thinking they are driven to make money and be successful, but this is not what self-motivation is really about. A truly emotionally intelligent person motivates themselves without thinking about money, power, praise, or acknowledgment because they don't need that to fuel their desire to go after what they want. When it comes to conflict resolution and self-motivation, you have to truly want to solve a conflict and not be afraid to bring up the difficult topic. Be proactive rather than procrastinating. Use your drive and ambition to help you persevere during the conflict. Here are some ways to help you build your emotional intelligence:

Surround Yourself with Positive People and Environments

Everyone knows that being negative only attracts more negativity into your life. When you surround yourself with positive people or highly motivated like-minded individuals, your self-motivation will increase significantly and your perspective will be more positive and hopeful. The biggest difference between a negative individual and a positive individual is that a positive person will come up with solutions not just point out the problems, while a negative person will come up with excuses not to solve problems and focus on the negative aspects of the issue. A positive person will see the good in every bad situation while a pessimistic person will always view the negative.

Do Not Overthink

Most overthinkers are people who listen too much to their inner critic or are perfectionists. When you are working on something that you need to think about, it is instinctive to analyze every aspect of it if we set our expectations too high. Not everything needs to be perfect. Ask for feedback, but don't obsess about it. It is a proven fact that perfectionists often fail because they try too hard at excellence instead of just getting something done to an acceptable level of quality. For example, a project result may be perfect, but it took too much time and went beyond the scope and was over-budget.

Track Your Success

Throughout our lives, we achieve great things but rarely get noticed or reward ourselves due to the lack of acknowledgment by others. However, a self-motivator recognizes these achievements and rewards themselves once they complete a task they have been working on. Over time, these rewards and successes will build up, so add these to your track record. A year later, you can look back at what you have accomplished, and this will continue to motivate you to keep going forward.

Be Helpful

Science says that the most empowering thing you can do to lift your spirits is to help others. Regardless of whether they are richer or poorer than you, when you help someone, it sends happy hormones to your brain, which makes you more motivated. For example, if someone comes to you and they are sad or need to vent, naturally you are going to want to cheer them up. By cheering them up through motivational and positive speech, you will feel better as well. This positive energy results in more self-motivation to continue your path towards success.

To gain emotional intelligence you need to be self-motivated and strive to achieve positive outcomes. You need the motivation to stay on track and build healthy habits such that emotional intelligence tools such as self-regulation and empathy come easier to you.

How Self-Regulation Decreases Conflict and How to Develop it

Think of self-regulation like self-control. It's the ability to process your emotions and calm them in conflict situations. It is another aspect of managing your emotions. Self-regulation first requires self-awareness. Self-awareness allows you to notice when you are angry or disappointed. Self-regulation gives you the functionality to calm yourself down before you escalate a conflict. Building your self-regulation skills increases your emotional intelligence and helps you make rational decisions, which is essential in conflict management.

In chapter five, you learned about self-awareness and what triggers your emotions. With self-regulation, once you know what triggers or upsets you, you can more effectively manage your emotions and their contribution to a conflict. When you learn self-regulation, you can:

- Delay your emotional responses.

- Develop efficient ways to calm yourself.

- Reflect on your thoughts.

- Understand the emotions of others.

- Regain composure.

Some self-regulating strategies are:

Become Open to Change

Narrow-minded people are so lost in their own world that they are unwilling to see the value in another person's opinion. When you are open-minded, you can manage change and variety in your life more easily than if you are closed-minded. For example, someone who self-regulates well is open to spontaneity and resilient to change if they need to be. For example, if you got demoted in your job, your heightened emotions might make you confrontational with your boss. This lack of self-regulation could escalate the situation even further, possibly resulting in you losing your job entirely.

Practice Self-Discipline

Self-discipline is when you can avoid temptations and get a job or task done on your own without anyone else pushing you to complete it. It's being able to define your weaknesses and work towards improving them but not seeing them as a barrier or roadblock in your success. Persistence and control are the foundations of self-regulating your emotions and conquering internal weaknesses. Self-disciplined people have higher emotional intelligence and are more focused on how they can accomplish what they need to in life. This promotes the chances of resolving conflict because self-discipline helps to keep attention on what really matters.

Talk Back to Your Inner Critic

Part of self-regulating is being able to talk back to your inner critic and reframe your negative thoughts. For example, if someone says you are not good at being creative or have poor communication skills, you may start to believe what they say about you. However, if you practice talking back to these thoughts, you can regulate how you feel about yourself and others. Eventually, the negative things people say, and the negative things you say to yourself won't bother you anymore, and you will be able to counter these thoughts with positive arguments. You can practice this by stating positive mantras to yourself every morning and visualizing success.

Breathe Under Pressure

Self-regulation requires being able to stay calm in a high pressure environment. For example, if you work in a fast-paced business, you will feel under pressure to do your best and move quickly. Self-regulation is about managing your self-awareness skills so that you can keep your composure in front of other people. Effective breathing allows us to address every situation with calm and composure. We talked about breathing in previous chapters, and learned that deep, regular breathing has a calming effect and helps us to focus. Practice this by using breathing techniques and other relaxation methods such as meditation whenever you feel pressured.

Identify the Outcome

When you can think rationally about what the outcome of your actions will be during a time of conflict, you further develop the skill of self-regulating your emotions and behaviors. Since self-regulation relies on knowing yourself, your triggers and what upsets you, only you can choose the right approach to resolving conflict. Think before you act and consider the consequences of your actions. Self-regulation requires taking responsibility for your contribution to a problem and finding ways to resolve it efficiently. This requires an awareness of what the optimal outcome of the situation is.

How Empathy Can Resolve Conflict

Empathy is the foundation of emotional intelligence. Emotional intelligence is about understanding your own emotions while recognizing the feelings of others. Empathy is the ability to put yourself in other people's shoes and see their side of things. Highly empathetic people feel the pain of others around them. For example, if your friend is sad, you might feel sad too. If your family member is angry, you might feel some of their anger "rub off on you". So, what does empathy have to do with conflict resolution?

While some people are aware of the emotions of others, some individuals cannot be empathetic. Conflict resolution requires you to see someone's point of view in order to help resolve the problem effectively. So, how do we learn to be more empathetic?

Push Your Limits

Doing uncomfortable or unfamiliar things teaches us to evolve personally, adapt to change and handle whatever conflict comes at us. By learning something new, such as playing a musical instrument or painting, or doing something hard like exercising or meeting new people, you will be more relaxed, humble, and skilled. Humility is a critical factor in developing empathy. Push your limits so that you can grow as a person.

Ask for Constructive Criticism

Part of learning to be empathetic is understanding how others view you and your weaknesses so that you can work on them for the benefit of others. Check in with your closest friends or people who know the real you and ask them how you respond to conflict or relationship issues. If someone tells you that you are great at helping out but bad at listening, then you know that you need to work on your listening skills.

Check in Often

The opposite of empathy is caring only for your own benefit, which shows that you are selfish or self-centered. To break this habit of always wanting to talk about yourself or do things that only help you, make a conscious effort to check in with the people you care about. Instead of calling someone for help, call someone to see if they could use an extra hand. Rather than asking someone to hang out for the intention of wanting something in return, call and see if you can take them for lunch or coffee just because you want to hear what is new in their life.

See Someone Else's Point of View

Although seeing someone else's perspective might be challenging for some people, making a conscious decision to really listen to someone else's point of view increases your empathy skills. When engaging in conversation, really listen to what the other person is telling you and think about how you would feel, what you would think, and what you would do if you were in their situation.

Keep Your Judgment at Bay

Say no to judgment. Just because you wouldn't do something that someone else is telling you that they did doesn't mean you are smarter than them. Everyone has their own reasons for why they do what they do. Judgment is the opposite of empathy and should be left at the door when practicing how to be more empathetic, and when trying to resolve conflict.

Ask Empathetic Questions

When engaging in conversation, show that you want to know more and that you are enthusiastic to hear their side by asking questions related to the topic. For example, if you don't know anything about dog training, but someone else is venting about their career, they might say that they had to train a misbehaved dog. If you cannot relate to them because of your dislike for dogs, disinterest in the career, or other personal views, you can start asking questions. Some empathetic questions might include, "How did you feel when the dog jumped on you? Why did you choose this career if it's so difficult? What is the worst day you have had, and how did you deal with it? What are the parts of the job you most enjoy?" By learning more about what another person feels and experiences, you can start to relate more to their situation.

You will develop empathy by putting these skills into practice and by being dedicated to the experience of personal growth. Empathy is not just a sign of high emotional intelligence but also a top sign of leadership and influential capabilities. Empathy can help you progress in many aspects of your life because it helps you relate to others on a higher level, and when we truly relate to others, we are less likely to have conflict with them.

Chapter Summary

Developing the four aspects of emotional intelligence we have discussed can dramatically affect your chances of resolving a conflict. Having a high emotional intelligence means that you can address the

101

situation, see from another's point of view, be empathetic to others and regulate your own emotions so that conflict does not escalate any further than it needs to.

In this chapter, you learned:

- What emotional intelligence is.

- How to increase your emotional intelligence.

- What self-motivation is and why it's important.

- What self-regulation is and how to develop it to resolve conflict.

- What empathy is and how to use it to resolve a dispute.

In the next chapter, you will learn how to make peace with conflict, even if the conflict cannot be resolved. You will understand constructive confrontation and how it relates to the many aspects of making peace with argumentative and narrow-minded people.

CHAPTER EIGHT

Conflict Resolution Technique 06 - The Strategy of Peace

In this chapter, you will learn the strategy of making peace. The ultimate goal of conflict resolution is a peaceful conclusion. A resolution where all parties receive an equitable outcome and have a deeper understanding of each other is what we strive to achieve. Regardless of what strategies are used, or how successful it is, in the end, the goal is to end the conflict. Making peace during or after a conflict requires that you effectively use positive solutions that are based on mutual understanding. As you strive towards a peaceful outcome to your conflicts, there are many tools you can use to create opportunities for resolution. The tools are based on constructive confrontation, the realization that you don't always have to be right, and how to know when to walk away gracefully.

Constructive Confrontation

Approach the conflict situation by creating a constructive confrontation opportunity. Constructive confrontation happens when you can communicate with the other party that you realize there is a conflict and you want to resolve it. Approach the other party with sincerity in your words and your heart. Use non-threatening body language. Start with taking responsibility for your contribution to the conflict. Be clear that you want to understand their perspective, come to a mutual agreement and make peace. Here are some tools you can use before and during a constructive confrontation event:

Observe the Situation

As you learned in chapter six, triple position is taking a step back and looking at the conflict as a whole while still considering the needs of each party. Take a step back and consider each aspect of the conflict. What is the root of the conflict? What is contributing to its escalation? What is the position of each party? Is there a common ground? Is this a safe appropriate space to have this constructive confrontation? Is there enough time to have a good talk? Is the other party argumentative, upset, or hostile? What kind of body language is being expressed by the parties? Are they mirroring your body language? Are they expressing body language that is closed off or angry? What does the vibe in the room feel like?

Use your emotional intelligence and observation skills to gather information that will assist you in developing a strategy for the situation. Regulate your emotions and be objective so that you can proceed calmly. When dealing with conflict, it is always best to talk face-to-face so that you can observe the situation fully.

Identify All Your Options

In order to identify all of your options, use the information you collected while observing the situation. Objectively consider different approaches to the constructive confrontation. Go over various scenarios in your head. Use what you know about the situation, the issues, and the other party to imagine what would happen if you used one approach, then imagine what would happen if you used a different approach. What words are they most likely to listen to? Do you need to make adjustments or accommodations to increase the chance of a successful outcome? Should you be sitting or standing? Should you be alone or in a public place? Think about what the potential outcomes are for every potential scenario you can think of. For example, consider these scenarios. If you are standing and they are sitting, and you say, "I think you're wrong about something and I want to talk about it," it is unlikely to go well. There is a chance the person will feel intimidated and say okay, allowing you to start with the conversation focused on you. There is a greater chance that the person will feel that you are overbearing, blaming them for something, and get upset or angry. However, if you were to start with both of you sitting, and you said, "I think we had a misunderstanding about something, and I'd like to talk about it," there is a good chance that the person will be receptive to the conversation and interested in resolving the misunderstanding. Identifying your options gives you the opportunity to choose the best potential solution. Consider the various options you have. Rank them as plan A, B and C just in case the person does not respond in the way you anticipated and you need to try another approach.

Confirm Understanding

Sometimes, to resolve conflict, it is best to confirm your understanding of everyone's point of view, and how they are similar or different. The most important thing about making peace is developing mutual understanding. Let the other party know that you realize there is a problem, and that you want to understand their point of view. Ask them to explain their perspective on the conflict, and listen carefully to what they say. Confirm what you believe they have said, and ask them if it is correct. Ask questions if you are unsure about anything. Validate their answer rather than immediately comparing it to your point of view. Thank them for helping you understand. It is then okay to say something like, "I think I understand your point of view better now. Is it okay if I explain my point of view and then maybe we can talk about the similarities and differences in our opinions?" Once you have exchanged points of view, you will both have an opportunity to recognize that the opinion of the other person is valid even though it is different from yours. If they are open to discussion, compare both of your points of view and talk about your common ground if there is any. Give feedback about their opinions, and ask for feedback about yours. Try to stick to facts rather than stating personal views, or at least be clear about what is fact and what is opinion. Talk openly about what exactly is the root of the conflict.

Reminisce on Past Success (NOT Past Mistakes)

All too often, we resort to bringing up past mistakes, which can make someone automatically defensive. Instead, you can point out the positive things that have been said and done before. Relate these to the situation you are in now or state how a conflict was solved amicably between you in the past. Talking about past successes may assist you to diffuse the conflict in a healthy, peaceful way. For example, if someone says, "I am mad because you don't understand, and you never have." You can make them feel more comfortable and redirect the conversation by responding in a calm tone and saying, "I understand that those are your feelings right now. I want to remind you that it worked really well when we agreed to XXX and we followed through. That helped us to understand each other. Working this out is important to me." Discuss how you were able to successfully understand each other when certain words, phrases, body language, time of day, location, etc. were used. Discuss how it feels when you use language that is blaming or hurtful. Choose to have a positive conversation. Agree to exchange points of view and have a constructive conversation about the successful resolution of your current conflict. Talk about what has worked for you in the past, so that you can apply any lessons learned from those situations.

Allow Time for Thought Processing and Effective Responses

Many times, during a conflict, we are impatient to hear a response to what we have said, so we pressure the individual to respond right away. All that does is cause more conflict because it heightens anxiety or hostility. This can also often result in saying things we don't really mean. Things may escalate quickly, and violence may even occur if someone is pushed too far. We are so anxious to get to the end that we push too hard, and don't take time to really consider what is being said. Instead, you should both take your time to calmly present your points, listen to the other person, think carefully about what was said, and discuss a clear path forward. Do not let your haste to be out of the uncomfortable situation compromise your need to take the time for clear composed thought and reflection.

Take Breaks

If you feel yourself getting flustered, or notice that the opposing party is agitated, suggest that you both take a break from the conversation. Ask to grab a coffee for you both, or suggest to change the subject to something lighter for now, with an intent to return to it later. However, do not forget to come back to it when you are both feeling better because avoiding or ignoring conflict will likely make it worse when the dispute resumes at a later date.

Constructive confrontation is about letting go of all judgment and making sure that you get involved entirely and personally in the conversation. Making peace requires you to be open to working out your conflict to the benefit of both parties, even if the only benefit is both parties walking away from the dispute. If you are in a conflict, take the initiative and actively seek out the opportunity to resolve it. Sometimes constructive confrontation is hard because you are too close to the person you are in conflict with. To be constructive in your approach, you have to look at situations from every perspective, including objectively like a therapist or a mentor would. Identify how you feel, what this person means to you, and decide if you can look at it from a triple position. Not all conflicts are resolved, but all conversations must come to an end eventually. When trying to end a heated discussion, try suggesting the last tool, taking a break, until you are both calm and can think rationally.

You Don't Always Need to Be Right

Competitive people are the ones who are the most argumentative because they need to get their point across and will not settle until others agree they are right. Does this sound like you or someone you know? If it's someone you know, sometimes just not saying anything argumentative can make all the difference. You might say, "You seem to be convinced it's true, so I will think about it." All you can control is yourself and your response, so why risk an argument if you already know that this person has to be right and will never back down?

If you are the competitive one, it may be best to consider the questions below so that you don't become your own worst enemy. Some of the most important lessons you can learn are: you don't always have to be right, some arguments aren't worth winning, the fault may actually be yours, you may have misunderstood, or maybe you are being mean or prideful. Always be willing to take responsibility for your own role in a conflict.

Am I Right or Am I Being Prideful?

The truth of the matter is, you may think you are right, but in reality, maybe you are just being overly opinionated, prideful and self-centered. Having opinions is not bad; however, when you mix it with a

109

competitive nature and bad conflict resolution skills, you may not be able to get along with people. What if it matters more how you handle conflict with others than whether you are more correct than they are? Maybe you have the drive and confidence to speak out, and you believe you know what you are talking about. What if you are actually wrong? Try considering how many times you have been right. Is it all the time, or do you only think you are right all the time? Maybe people are just tired of arguing with you. Constantly trying to prove to others that you are right is prideful.

Sometimes having to be right stems from a competitive nature. It may result from not being heard by others or from feeling neglected when we were young. Competitiveness makes us feel better about ourselves because when we win arguments we feel successful and like a winner. Being competitive does not contribute to effective conflict resolution. Don't be so competitive. Be cooperative. Next time you are confronted with a conflict, don't focus on winning or being right. Consider letting someone else be right and see how you feel. If you feel emotionally crushed, or unreasonably angry when you don't win an argument, it might be best to look into the underlying causes of this. Go talk to a counselor to identify your core patterns so that you don't miss out on future opportunities to build closer bonds with others.

Is it Worth Winning the Argument?

Determine if an argument is worth winning, and if it is, understand what the cost will be to your relationship, circumstance, or safety. Maybe it's not worth winning. It's okay to let someone else have their way. Look at your environment and analyze the situation. Where are you? Who are you talking to? What is the argument about? Do you really need to win? If you win do you risk losing a friend or loved one because they are so hurt by your approach to winning? Do you risk offending or angering someone who is in a position of power over you? There is a big difference between arguing with your boss about their reaction to your finished project as opposed to arguing with your friends about a local political issue. During a debate with your friends, it's okay to try to vigorously win a friendly argument; however, even a minor disagreement with your boss might cost you your job. A dispute with your wife over how to parent may not be the right fight to try to win; however, a disagreement over a guys' night out might be okay. If someone suggests you do something unsafe together and you don't want to, it is very important that you win the argument. If they suggest you do something boring and you don't want to, it doesn't really have a large consequence who wins.

What Caused the Conflict?

Instead of arguing with your friends, your spouse, your boss, or a family member, think back to what caused this current argument or others in the past. Is this a recurring argument or a new disagreement? Is it a difference of opinion on something intangible, or is there an opportunity to resolve the conflict based on facts? Is there something to be gained or lost that is fueling the conflict? Identify the underlying cause of this confrontation so you can find a constructive way to deal with it. If you are working together to resolve the conflict, make sure you both agree on what the root cause of the conflict is.

Are You Being Spiteful or Hurtful?

When we are wrapped up in the moment, we can become spiteful by bringing up past events or saying deliberately hurtful things. We don't usually intentionally try to hurt the other party; however, because we know them, we also know what buttons to press to get a reaction. Ask yourself if you are deliberately provoking the other person. Are you saying things that are mean or upsetting to them? Being hurtful towards the other party will escalate a dispute and possibly end your relationship.

When Conflict Cannot Be Resolved

Sometimes people just can't agree and the discussion has to end. Making peace doesn't always have to mean that the conflict has been resolved to the satisfaction of all parties. Sometimes making peace can mean just agreeing to disagree and parting company with no hard feelings. In these circumstances, you need to understand when it's appropriate to just let things go. For example, if the other party will not let go of their point, and no matter what you say, it will only lead to an escalation of the dispute, you might choose not to say anything more.

Depending on what type of conflict you are in, and who you are speaking to, it's best to know when you should talk things out, when to be silent for a while, and when to let it go completely. So, how are we to be sure when to talk things out or not? When should you just make peace with the situation and move on? Consider the following:

- Is the conflict big or small?

- Will it matter in a weeks' time or change anything if it isn't settled?

- What are the consequences of winning, losing, or walking away?

- Is it worth losing the person you are speaking with?

- Is it worth losing yourself in the moment?

- Are you hungry, tired, emotional, or is something else contributing to the dispute?

Sometimes it's easy to make peace. If the battle is something small and silly, make some humor out of it and say, "Gee, this is quite silly and has gotten out of hand don't you think?" However, when you make this bold statement, make sure it is something small like an argument over cutting potatoes or which movie to watch. Sometimes, we don't notice that small things may be contributing to our behavior. If we are hungry, tired, prideful, or selfish in the moment we can escalate a minor issue into a hostile conflict. When an issue is minor, be quick to say, "This issue isn't worth arguing about." Observe the situation objectively and then decide if you should just stop arguing and make peace.

Ending A Conflict Gracefully

Ending a conflict gracefully requires you to end on a positive or neutral note. It also means accepting the outcome without holding a grudge or hard feelings. Many people view conflict as a problem but rarely see it as an opportunity for positive change and inner growth.

113

Although the conflict may seem to be something negative, conflict is actually a positive thing because it helps us define who we are and who someone else is on a deeper level. You have not ended the conflict gracefully if you haven't really ended the argument. If you are just holding on to the hostility with a plan to argue later, or you are planning to avoid the person in the future, or one of you ends up leaving disappointed and unheard, then you haven't resolved anything. Resolving conflict gracefully means knowing what to say, when to stop talking and when to walk away. Here's a recap of some of the essential skills for making peace and ending a conflict gracefully:

- Keep negative thoughts to yourself. Don't say them out loud.

- Focus on positive common ground.

- Practice effective listening skills.

- Validate the other person's feelings.

- Stay on topic.

- Bring up what has worked in the past

- Don't say hurtful things.

- Focus on the solution, not on being right.

- Remember why you value having this person in your life.

- Stay away from making it a competition.

This chapter is about what to do when you can't resolve a conflict but you want to make peace. It's about how to end the conflict and walk away peacefully. This may take both actions and words. Sometimes the conflict escalates because of the words you are using. Let's look at some examples of how you can say positive, constructive things and work towards making peace.

"I needed to hear that, thank you. I will keep that in mind."

Stating this validates the person you are talking to. Even if you don't agree or relate to their opinion or view, it shows that you are trying to understand, and that you will put more thought into it. It helps them know that they are being heard and that you are open to their point of view.

"I have something to say. Is now a good time to tell you about it?"

This statement can be said in the middle of an argument or before you start a potentially difficult conversation. It lets the other person know that you have an opinion and need to be heard, but that you need their full attention. At times, it can also make someone aware that they might be getting off-topic or venting too much, and that it's your turn to speak.

"What do you think about us searching for some facts?"

As mentioned previously, some arguments are all about being right. In some cases, it is possible to find or provide proof of which position is actually correct. In this situation, both parties must agree to respect the outcome of the fact finding.

"I am interpreting what you said like XXX. Is this correct? Please help me understand if I am wrong."

115

Effective verbal communication includes re-phrasing what the speaker has said to you so that you are sure you understand it. If you aren't clear about what they mean, you can ask them to explain themselves or provide examples. This shows that you are trying to get the full story without jumping to conclusions.

"I am not very comfortable with that idea, can we come up with something else?"

Stating this shows that even though you heard what they are saying, you aren't on board with it but still want to work together to solve the problem. This is an effective way to open the door for using negotiation and persuasion techniques which you learned about previously.

Thinking before you speak and saying constructive positive things can significantly increase your chances of walking away from the conflict with a solution or at least with the peace of mind that you tried your best.

How to Apologize

You must be thinking, "I know how to apologize, why is this even a heading?" It's because apologies can come off as aggressive or ingenuine if you just apologize because that's what the other party wants in order to settle the conflict. The number one rule of apologizing is that you must mean it. It must be sincere.

The only way to show that you are sincere is to genuinely think about the conflict and be truly sorry you hurt then. You must also be willing to not do what you said sorry for in the future. For example,

116

maybe your spouse gets upset with you because you don't fold the laundry or help around the house. You might have your own opinion that you do help out and that it goes unnoticed. However, to end the argument before it begins, you might just automatically say sorry. Then you do it again because your first apology wasn't genuine. You never intended to actually change your behavior. You said sorry in order to end the conflict at that moment in time. With this type of apology, sorry soon starts to mean nothing, and the other person is likely to lose trust in you and your sincerity.

Here is what a genuine apology sounds like:

"I can see that I hurt you. I am sorry."

Make sure that when you apologize, it comes from within, and that you genuinely mean it. Be prepared to explain how they were hurt and what you are sorry for. Otherwise, an apology will seem ingenuine, offhand and dishonest. The opposing party may not be able to trust you when you actually are sorry in the future. Here are some examples of what an insincere or ingenuine apology sounds like:

- "Whatever, I am sorry."

- "If you want an apology from me, here it is, I am sorry."

- "I am sorry that you are so XXX."

- "You are right, I guess I will never learn to please you."

- "It's all my fault. I am such a horrible person."

117

So, what exactly makes an apology genuine? The best apologies happen when you:

- Do not rush it and explain why you are sorry for what you have done.

- Take responsibility for the part you played in the dispute and don't expect or ask for an apology back.

- Do not justify what you have done, explain why you did what you did and acknowledge that it was the wrong approach.

- Promise to make the changes necessary to ensure it doesn't happen again.

- Ask for forgiveness.

- Follow through with any promises made.

Acknowledgment

A proper and respectful apology is interpreted and received better if you acknowledge that there is a dispute and that you are not happy about being in conflict with the person. Summarize the dispute from the third position perspective. When you are being sincere, acknowledge the dispute, your role in the dispute, and have thought about the entire situation, you can quickly clarify what is wrong and what you will do differently next time.

Responsibility

Some people are too wrapped up in the heat of the moment to consider their own actions or how they contributed to escalating the conflict. Taking responsibility means admitting what you did to contribute to the conflict, and letting the other person know. To practice taking responsibility you can:

- Examine the scenario without putting blame on the other person or parties.

- Consider everyone's contribution including your own.

- Apologize for what you have done.

- Learn from your mistakes.

- Choose a peaceful approach.

Taking responsibility for your actions doesn't have to result in an apology. Just the fact that you have realized what you have done wrong means that you are one step closer to resolving conflict peacefully.

Understanding and Empathy

After you have acknowledged the dispute and taken responsibility for how your own thoughts and actions contributed to the argument, show empathy and compassion by thinking and stating how you believe the other person feels. True understanding may not happen until after the conflict ends, and you've had a chance to think about it.

When apologizing, make sure you have put thought into your apology and remember to listen to what the other person has said. Give them a chance to respond to the apology. Your intention may be to be forgiven, but this doesn't always happen right away. Sometimes accepting that someone needs more time is the only way to resolve an

119

issue for the time being. Don't forget to forgive yourself. Look at yourself in the mirror, apologize to yourself and forgive yourself for the way you handled things. Holding onto anger and hate or betrayal can cause anxiety and deepened stress. Forgiveness is not always possible, but if you walk away from an unresolved conflict satisfied with your own approach, you can continue to learn and develop conflict resolution skills in the future.

Chapter Summary

Whether you are constructively criticizing, confronting, or resolving, peaceful conflict resolution is about learning positive ways to end conflict gracefully. When conflict cannot be resolved, it's best to be quiet and listen, identify your contribution, and let go of wanting to be right. When saying sorry is about ending a conflict just to end it, you are ingenuine. When you say sorry because you actually are, you are more likely to have a peaceful end to the difficult situation, even if you don't fully resolve the conflict. Now you know techniques to effectively and peacefully end a conflict even if there is no true resolution, or you are not forgiven.

In this chapter, you learned:

- What constructive confrontation is.

- When to end conflict and when not to.

- When to let unresolved conflict go.

- How to speak in a way that will lead to a graceful end to a difficult conversation.

- How to apologize authentically.

In the next chapter, you will learn how to open your mind and rethink problems and conflict. By reframing your point of view and using conflict to positively change your life, you can master yet another tool available to you as you strive to resolve conflict in your life.

CHAPTER NINE

Conflict Resolution Technique 07 - The Power of Keeping an Open Mind

Keeping an open mind is all about perspective, alternate interpretations and reframing your way of thinking. The reason this technique is so beneficial is that often our minds are so set in our own thinking patterns that we can forget that someone else sees it differently. As you have learned throughout this book, having a competitive nature or a closed-off attitude can heighten conflict. Keeping an open mind influences our behavior and sets up how we approach conflict and discussion. The reason most people are comfortable with keeping thoughts to themselves or having a closed mind is that during the conflict, they feel uncomfortable or defensive and a closed-off attitude makes them feel secure. Without realizing it, this type of behavior contributes to an escalation of the dispute or argument. You might ask, "Why would I allow myself to be vulnerable if I feel threatened? If the other party in the conflict continues to put me down and doesn't make me feel comfortable, then why should I try?"

123

In this state of a closed-off mind, we might wait for an apology or think that the other party has to make the first move before we are willing to consider resolving the conflict. In some cases, this approach is healthy if you feel the other party has truly wronged you and you need space and time to consider the situation. However, before thinking they need to make the first move, consider your relationship and the overall perspective of the conflict. Take a step back and evaluate the whole scenario before making a sudden and permanent decision. Would having an open mind make it easier to understand the problem? Are you ready to consider other perspectives? Is there something you can do to understand the situation better? What can you control, and what can you not control regarding this matter? Perhaps you wonder why you should open up when you don't feel like it? Perhaps you are scared of getting hurt. That's natural. There are many benefits to opening your mind to the perspectives of others and to the potential of a positive outcome.

Here are some of the benefits:

- You may learn that you are not the only one who might be feeling threatened.

- You might discover that their behavior is stemming from fear.

- They might not realize they can't control themselves during a conflict.

- You stay non-judgmental by keeping an open mind.

- You may be able to decrease the level of hostility which will improve the chance of resolving the conflict.

In chapter seven, you learned the power of emotional intelligence and how it can help you resolve conflicts. Using empathy can help you understand that being closed-off will only escalate things further because you are closed-off to what the other person is thinking and feeling. That's not to say that your feelings and opinions don't matter. However, the ultimate cause of the rising conflict could be that you both feel the same way but don't know how to express it. So, how do you fix this? Consciously keep an open mind and reframe your thinking. Remember the importance of effective listening strategies. Keeping an open mind requires active listening skills.

Reframing Your Mind for Effective Conflict Resolution

The concept of reframing one's mind is to view things differently than you have been. In the previous chapters, you have learned the concept of empathy, which is to understand another's opinion and how they feel and think. Reframing your mind doesn't mean to look outside the box or think of the bigger picture. Reframing your mindset is the act of reshaping the way you see or view your own point of view to be receptive to the opinions of others. This allows us to expand and evolve our perspectives to include new information based on the perspectives of others.

Usually, when you go into a conflict you already have an interpretation of what the problem is, how to solve it, and where it came from. Only you can know your own thoughts and what you want to do about it. However, you don't truly understand what another feels and thinks. It could be completely different from what you have assumed.

125

With emotional intelligence tools such as empathy you can try your best to relate to the person or people you are in conflict with. Reframing your mind is not about looking at things from your own side differently, nor is it looking at things only from another's perspective. It's about understanding that you can look at the conflict in many ways and that there may be many valid and invalid components to everyone's point of view. One way of practicing reframing your mind is to get advice from different people who are not involved in the conflict.

One of the barriers to reframing your mind when it comes to a dispute is that during an argument, we revert back to first person perspective and get caught up in the desire to win. However, when you remain calm and keep your composure you can reframe your mindset and get a healthy view of the situation. You can reframe more than just your own thoughts. You can reframe the terms of the whole conflict by helping others to see the bigger perspective and the positive side of the situation. However, reframing and thus altering the outcome of a conflict requires you to first reframe your own state of mind. Strive to understand all aspects of the issue and then address the concern in a calm manner. Here are ways to reframe your mindset:

Underline the Root of the Issue

The first step to reframing your mind about the conflict is to identify what the underlying cause is. Many disputes escalate because we get caught up in the heat of the argument and focus on what's being said in that specific moment. However, we sometimes don't realize that the things that are being said and done right now have nothing to do with the actual root of the crisis. For example, if your boss accuses you of not working as hard as everyone else and recommends that you pick up the slack, it may not be because you aren't working hard enough. The underlying cause may be that your boss is having a rough day or a rough patch in their own lives, and that they are taking it out on you. Alternatively, it may be true that you aren't working hard enough because you are tired from being up all night with the baby.

Reframe the Negative

Once you have figured out what the underlying cause of the dispute is, you can restate the negative and think more positively about the scenario. Some ways to do this are:

- Change the intensity of the conversation by speaking calmly and using non-threatening body language.

- Use empathy and compassion.

- Find out what might work for both parties.

- Find a positive thing that you can both agree on.

- Restate the problem to make sure you both understand.

- Redirect the discussion back to the underlying issue.

- Focus on a solution.

In order to effectively reframe the conflict with your boss you can apologize genuinely and explain that you are having a rough patch at home but will try your best to focus. Or, if your boss is having a rough day, you might politely say something like, "I'm sorry it seems that way to you. I've actually accomplished XXX today." Let your boss know that you are doing your best.

The main focus behind reframing is to shift your view or the other party's perspective about how the dispute feels to you or them and say something positive that will lead to a solution.

Viewing Conflict as a Positive

Almost all people who have been in conflict with another individual think of it as a bad thing. However, disputes and quarrels between you and someone else should not be looked at as a bad thing. As we talk about the root causes of conflict, part of reframing your mindset requires you to look at conflict as something healthy. Once your mind is in the right place, you can approach the dispute in the right way. Regardless of if conflict makes you feel angry, sad or disappointed, there are many reasons why conflict can be a positive thing in your life. As the saying goes, it always rains before you see a rainbow. Think of the conflict as the rain, and the resolution the rainbow.

Three types of growth can come from conflict and conflict resolution. Those are:

Personal Growth

Conflict helps you define your own deeper emotions and thoughts. This helps you to achieve enlightenment, accept change, and have a deeper understanding of yourself. We grow and evolve when we challenge ourselves and face conflict with an open mind.

128

Relational Growth

Conflict may exist with other people; however, the process of resolving conflict helps you grow both individually, and in relation to others by gaining a deeper understanding of how someone else thinks. When you work with others to build positive outcomes, your relationships will also develop in positive ways.

Structural Growth

Structural growth comes from your work environment. Conflict can sometimes happen at work. If we didn't have conflict at work, we might never really understand the extent of our responsibilities, what people around us think about our work, or what others need from us. We would not learn how to speak professionally, swallow our pride, and resolve conflicts with grace. These qualities might lead to getting recognized as a leader, or as someone who is resilient to change in a challenging workplace. We gain structural growth by learning how to succeed despite conflict.

Aside from these three types of growth and the opportunities we gain from experiencing conflict, there are many other reasons why conflict can be a good thing. Some of the reasons why conflict can be positive are that it:

- Provides us insight.

- Gives us the opportunity to express ourselves.

- Helps us evaluate our core needs.

- Teaches us responsibility and empathy.

129

- Makes us listen to understand.

- Shows us our own behaviors and unhealthy patterns.

- Turns something negative like a conflict into positive solutions by addressing needs.

- Allows us to work on our communication skills.

- Helps us identify our values and set clear boundaries.

- Promotes emotional balance and control.

- Allows us to view problems from the point of view of others.

When you look at it, conflict is a great thing, especially when your goal is to solve a problem and build positive relationships with others.

FINAL WORDS

The problem with conflict is that it's always around us. No matter where we go, what we do or how we think, conflict inevitably finds us. You may not be in conflict right now, but you have probably experienced it in the past. You are likely to experience conflict in the future. It is essential to have techniques and tools to recognize, defuse and resolve conflict.

Is conflict itself really the problem, or is it how we deal with it? As you have learned in this book, conflict resolution is about how you deal with conflict and change the ultimate outcome of the situation. There are healthy ways to deal with conflict, and there are negative ways to manage conflict. This book has shown you the ins and outs, the ups and downs, the negatives and positives of conflict and conflict resolution so that the next time you are confronted, you can handle it effectively.

Ask yourself what you can take away from reading this book. Think back to what your state of mind was like before reading this book and compare it to what you feel and believe now. Ask yourself what you know now that you didn't before. What is your contribution to the conflicts you have been involved in? How are you going to handle things differently? How can you learn about yourself and others? How can you find solutions that are mutually beneficial? These questions are good to ask and will lead to positive behaviors. Conflict cannot be avoided or ignored.

In the introduction, I assured you that you would gain a greater understanding of how to resolve conflict better and figure out what roles you play in escalating issues. Do you now have a deeper understanding of yourself as well as of others? Are there things you learned about yourself that you didn't know before? By now, you should have a different perspective on the disputes you have been a part of. You should also have a variety of techniques at your disposal that can assist with resolving the conflicts in your life.

In this book, you have learned seven different techniques to help you resolve conflict. By practicing and mastering these techniques you will achieve personal and professional growth and experience the benefits that conflict resolution skills bring to your life. Remember these techniques and use them the next time you are in a situation that requires conflict resolution skills.

Let's review the seven techniques again to ensure this book ends with our best advice to you.

1. Mastering the power of conversation through verbal communication tools.

2. Mastering the power of conversation through non-verbal communication tools.

3. Managing emotions.

4. Changing minds using persuasion and negotiation.

5. Developing emotional intelligence so that you can resolve conflict like a leader.

6. The strategy of peace.

7. The power of keeping an open mind.

My wish for you from this point forward is that you approach every challenge and conflict with grace and gratitude. Continue to practice our seven techniques, keep learning, and move towards growth in all aspects of your life. Now that you have effective tools to resolve conflict in your life, the possibilities are endless. Don't stop now, reach for your goals and dreams with confidence.

All the best,

Gerard Shaw

RESOURCES

- B. Spangler (2003) Reframing. Retrieved from
  https://www.beyondintractability.org/essay/joint_reframing

- Brenda (2016) The Awesome Communication Tool:
  Reframing. Retrieved from
  http://brendahooper.com/the-awesome-communication-tool-reframing/

- C. Childs (2019) 8 Steps to Continuous Self Motivation Even
  During the Difficult Times. Retrieved from,
  https://www.lifehack.org/articles/featured/8-steps-to-continuous-self-motivation.html

- D, Bellafiore (n.d.) Interpersonal Conflict and Effective
  Communication. Retrieved from
  http://www.drbalternatives.com/articles/cc2.html

- D, Prothrow-Stith (n.d.) Conflict Resolution: The Human
  Dimension. Retrieved from
  https://www.gmu.edu/programs/icar/ijps/vol3_1/burton.htm

- D, Stone, B Patton, and S. Heen (n.d.) Difficult Conversations:
  How To Discuss What Matters Most Handout. Retrieved from

https://www.mdmunicipal.org/DocumentCenter/View/3656/Difficult-Conversations-Handout?bidId

- D.W Johnson (2019) The Importance of Taking the Perspective of Others. Retrieved from https://www.psychologytoday.com/ca/blog/constructive-controversy/201906/the-importance-taking-the-perspective-others

- Dr. T, Alessandra (May 2018) Conflict Resolution Behaviors. Retrieved from
  https://assessments24x7.com/blog/conflict-resolution-behaviors/

- E. Katrina (2014) 7 Tips to Follow to End Any Argument Peacefully. Retrieved from
  https://www.realsimple.com/work-life/work-life-etiquette/sticky-situations/things-say-keep-peace

- H. Shorey (2017) Managing Relationship Conflict: Letting Go of Being Right. Retrieved from https://www.psychologytoday.com/ca/blog/the-freedom-change/201710/managing-relationship-conflict-letting-go-being-right

- J. Denny (2006) Constructive Confrontation. Retrieved from
  https://cmoe.com/blog/the-power-of-constructive-confrontation/

- J. Segal, M. Smith, L. Robinson, and G. Boose (2019) Nonverbal Communication. Retrieved from https://www.helpguide.org/articles/relationships-communication/nonverbal-communication.htm

- J.C. Williamson (2017) Effective Apologies Turn Conflict Aftermath into Healing Afterglow. Retrieved from https://www.huffpost.com/entry/effective-apologies-turn-b_11950994

- L Puhn (2017) 10 Things to Say to Keep the Peace. Retrieved from https://www.realsimple.com/work-life/work-life-etiquette/sticky-situations/things-say-keep-peace

- M, Clayton (2017) Roger Fisher, and William Ury: Principled Negotiation. Retrieved from https://www.pocketbook.co.uk/blog/2017/06/27/roger-fisher-william-ury-principled-negotiation/

- M, Dixit (2004) Theories of Conflict Resolution. Retrieved from http://www.ipcs.org/comm_select.php?articleNo=1531

- M. Carroll (2012) The Application of NLP Perceptual Positions. Retrieved from, https://www.nlpacademy.co.uk/articles/view/resolving_conflict_by_exploring_different_perspectives/

- Melissa (2018) The 5 Aspects of Emotional Intelligence and Why They Matter. Retrieved from
  https://awato.org/5-aspects-emotional-intelligence-matter/

- Nick (2016) POP for Safety. Retrieved from
  https://nicholas-davies.com/pop-for-safety/

- P. Scott (2016) The Power of Constructive Confrontation. Retrieved from
  https://cmoe.com/blog/the-power-of-constructive-confrontation/

- PON Staff (2019) Four Conflict Negotiation Strategies for Resolving Value-Based Disputes. Retrieved from
  https://www.pon.harvard.edu/daily/dispute-resolution/four-negotiation-strategies-for-resolving-values-based-disputes/

- R. Reece (n.d.) Emotional Intelligence and Conflict Management. Retrieved from
  http://emotionalintelligenceworkshops.com/emotional-intelligence-conflict-management.htm

- Rob (June 2014) 5 Stages of Conflict and Workplace Conflict Resolution. Retrieved from
  https://blog.udemy.com/stages-of-conflict/

- S, Amaresan (March 2019) 5 Conflict Management Styles for Every Personality Type. Retrieved from
  https://blog.hubspot.com/service/conflict-management-styles

- S, Kukreja (n.d.) Types of Conflict Situations. Available at: https://www.managementstudyhq.com/types-of-conflict-situations.html

- S, London (n.d.) The Power of Dialogue. Retrieved from http://scott.london/articles/ondialogue.html

- S. Campbell (2016) The Benefits of Conflict. Retrieved from https://www.entrepreneur.com/article/279778

- S. Kline (n.d.) 8 Ways to Improve Self- Regulation. Retrieved from http://preventchildabuse.org/wp-content/uploads/2016/10/8-Ways-to-Improve-Self-Regulation.pdf

- S.J. Scott (2019) What is Self-Awareness and How to Develop it. Retrieved from https://www.developgoodhabits.com/what-is-self-awareness/

- Stefan Jacobson (March 2017) The Benefits of Conflict Resolution. Retrieved from https://www.conovercompany.com/the-benefits-of-conflict-resolution/

- T. Coke (2015) The Power of an Open Mind. Retrieved from https://www.hrmagazine.co.uk/article-details/the-power-of-an-open-mind

- Unknown (2012) What Makes an Apology Authentic and Effective as a Resolution of Conflict? Retrieved from https://www.choiceconflictresolution.com/2012/10/31/what-makes-an-apology-authentic-and-effective-as-a-resolution-of-conflict/

- Unknown (2014) What is the Difference Between Negotiation and Persuasion? Retrieved from https://www.scotwork.com.au/negotiation-blog/2014/what-is-the-difference-between-negotiation-and-persuasion/

- Unknown (2015). Signs of Frustration. Retrieved from https://flowpsychology.com/signs-of-frustration/

- Unknown (2016) 8 Ways to Improve Your Empathy. Retrieved from https://andrewsobel.com/eight-ways-to-improve-your-empathy/

- Unknown (2017) 14 Ways to Approach a Conflict and Difficult Conversations at Work. Retrieved from https://www.forbes.com/sites/forbescoachescouncil/2017/07/17/14-ways-to-approach-conflict-and-difficult-conversations-at-work/#237397023cfd

- Unknown (2018) Why Conflict is Good. Retrieved from https://www.christianmuntean.com/why-conflict-is-good/

- Unknown (2019) Summary of Cooperation and Competition. Retrieved from: https://www.beyondintractability.org/artsum/deutsch-cooperation

- Unknown (August 2013) What is Conflict? - Understanding Conflict. Retrieved from http://www.typesofconflict.org/what-is-conflict/

- Unknown (n.d.) Conflict De-Escalation Techniques. Retrieved from https://vividlearningsystems.com/safety-toolbox/conflict-de-escalation-techniques

- Unknown (n.d.) Dynamic Risk Assessment - SAFER. Retrieved from http://www.conflictresolutionmanchester.com/risk-assessment.htm

- Unknown (n.d.) Life Skills Development Module Three: Conflict Management. Retrieved from https://wikieducator.org/Life_Skills_Development/Module_Three/Unit_3:_Conflict_Management/Elements_of_conflict

- Unknown (n.d.) Skills You Need - Effective Speaking. Retrieved from https://www.skillsyouneed.com/ips/effective-speaking.html

- Unknown (n.d.) Skills You Need - Verbal Communication Skills. Retrieved from https://www.skillsyouneed.com/ips/verbal-communication.html

- Unknown (n.d.) Summary of Difficult Conversations: How To Discuss What Matters Most. Retrieved from
  https://www.beyondintractability.org/bksum/stone-difficult

- Unknown (n.d.) Ten Persuasion Techniques. Retrieved from
  http://www.how-to-negotiate.com/ten-persuasion-techniques.html

- V. Greene (n.d.) Persuasive Tactics to Close Your Next Deal. Retrieved from

  https://www.neurosciencemarketing.com/blog/articles/persuasive-tactics.htm#

- VC. Nuance (n.d.) Deal with Anger in a Conflict Situation. Retrieved from

  https://visihow.com/Deal_with_Anger_in_a_Conflict_Situation

- Young Entrepreneur Council (2018). 14 Negative Body Language Signals and Speech Habits to Avoid. Retrieved from https://www.forbes.com/sites/theyec/2018/05/04/14-negative-body-language-signals-and-speech-habits-to-avoid/#1a6da62622f5

YOUR FREE GIFT IS HERE!

Thank you for purchasing this book. As a token and supplement to your new learnings and personal development journey, you will receive this booklet as a gift, and it's completely free.

This includes - as already announced in this book - a valuable resource of simple approach and actionable ideas to mastermind your own routine towards a more calm and confident way to tackle your everyday.

This booklet will provide you powerful insights on:

- How to formulate empowering habits that can change your life

- Masterminding your own Power of 3

- Just the 3 things you need to drastically change your life and how you feel about yourself

- How to boost your self-esteem and self-awareness

- Creating a positive feedback loop everyday

You can get the bonus booklet as follows:

To access the secret download page, open a browser window on your computer or smartphone and enter: bonus.gerardshaw.com

You will be automatically directed to the download page.

Please note that this bonus booklet may be available for download for a limited time only.

CPSIA information can be obtained
at www.ICGtesting.com
Printed in the USA
LVHW082227050421
683402LV00013B/25